Success and Sanity on the College Campus

A Guide for Parents

Diana Trevouledes and Ingrid Grieger

ROWMAN & LITTLEFIELD EDUCATION
A division of
ROWMAN & LITTLEFIELD PUBLISHERS, INC.
Lanham • New York • Toronto • Plymouth, UK

Published by Rowman & Littlefield Education
A division of Rowman & Littlefield Publishers, Inc.
A wholly owned subsidiary of The Rowman & Littlefield Publishing Group, Inc.
4501 Forbes Boulevard, Suite 200, Lanham, Maryland 20706
www.rowman.com

10 Thornbury Road, Plymouth PL6 7PP, United Kingdom

Copyright © 2012 by Diana Trevouledes and Ingrid Grieger
First paperback edition 2014

All rights reserved. No part of this book may be reproduced in any form or by any electronic or mechanical means, including information storage and retrieval systems, without written permission from the publisher, except by a reviewer who may quote passages in a review.

British Library Cataloguing in Publication Information Available

Library of Congress Cataloging-in-Publication Data
The hardback edition of this book was previously cataloged by the Library of Congress as follows :

Trevouledes, Diana.
Success and sanity on the college campus : a guide for parents / Diana Trevouledes and Ingrid Grieger.
p. cm.
Summary: "In this book, parents will learn about the most significant factors to be considered in making a wise decision about college selection, about the process of making a successful transition to college, about the potential pitfalls inherent in college life, and the warning signs and risk factors for psychological distress. In addition, parents will become acquainted with the protective factors and the resources available on the campus that enhance academic success and persistence to graduation, as well as emotional health and well-being"— Provided by publisher.
1. Education, Higher—Parent participation—United States—Handbooks, manuals, etc. 2. College choice—United States—Handbooks, manuals, etc. 3. Universities and colleges—United States—Admission—Handbooks, manuals, etc. 4. College student orientation—United States—Handbooks, manuals, etc. 5. College students—United States—Psychology. I. Grieger, Ingrid Zachary. II. Title.
LB2350.5.T74 2012
378.1'98—dc23
2012022928

ISBN: 978-1-61048-101-4 (cloth : alk. paper)
ISBN: 978-1-61048-102-1 (pbk : alk. paper)
ISBN: 978-1-61048-103-8 (electronic)

∞™ The paper used in this publication meets the minimum requirements of American National Standard for Information Sciences Permanence of Paper for Printed Library Materials, ANSI/NISO Z39.48-1992.

Printed in the United States of America

This book is dedicated to parents and students everywhere, to my family, my patients, and the memory of William Trevouledes.

—D.T.

For all of the college students it has been my honor to counsel, train, teach, and mentor, and for two special college students of the future, Taylor Rachel Zachary, class of 2031, and Ryan Eliza Zachary, class of 2034.

—I.G.

Contents

Introduction   1

1   The Role of the Parent in Promoting Emotional Wellness: A Basic Framework   9
2   Helping Your Child with College Selection and Preparation   17
3   The Transition to College and How Parents Can Help   37
4   Today's Campus Environment: What Parents Should Know about the Realities of College Life   57
5   Recognizing Signs of Psychological Problems, Chemical Dependency, and Addictive Behavior: What Parents Need to Know   77
6   Campus Services and Resources   105
7   Promoting Emotional Wellness and Student Success: Some Approaches That Work   119

Conclusion   135

Notes   139

Index   147

About the Authors   151

Introduction

Congratulations! Your son or daughter is a currently enrolled college student or is college bound. What an achievement for both you and your child!

As a parent, you have created a home environment of support, encouragement, and intellectual stimulation, which has instilled perseverance, a striving for excellence, and a value for learning in your child. In turn, your son or daughter has worked hard and has been diligent and conscientious in attaining the coveted goal of college admission. The reward for so much hard work and sacrifice on both your parts should be a joyful and successful college experience. Attending college should be the adventure of a lifetime, the opportunity to immeasurably grow intellectually and personally, to be exposed to a wealth of new ideas, to engage in new experiences, to meet new people, and ultimately to be launched into the world of work or graduate school.

For many students, their time in college *is* a wonderful journey, characterized by productivity, success, and extraordinary growth. These students enter college as enthusiastic and eager, but somewhat unformed, adolescents and emerge as competent, educated, focused, and resilient young adults. However, increasingly, college students are facing formidable challenges that create stumbling blocks to the successful completion of their college education and to their ongoing personal growth and development.

As college and university counseling center counselors and directors, as faculty members and researchers, we have collectively been engaged with college students and with the campus community for several decades. As such, we have had front-row seats to the escalating challenges that have emerged on the college campus, particularly over the last ten to fifteen years. Further, our observations as campus insiders have been confirmed by the reported experiences of our colleagues across the country, by high-visibility campus tragedies, and by a wealth of empirical data. These data include the results from counseling center directors' surveys, student surveys, and our own internal client databases, as well as epidemiological studies regarding such issues as suicidality and substance abuse among college students.[1]

These multiple sources of information indicate that some of the significant challenges confronting current college students include the following:

- A mental health crisis on the campus, characterized by a larger population of students with psychological problems and an increasing level of severity regarding the nature of these problems, including clinical depression, anxiety disorders, eating disorders, self-injury, chemical dependency, suicidality, and thought disorders.
- Higher levels of overall stress, emotional exhaustion, depression, and thoughts of suicide reported in the general college student population.[2]
- A reduction in external controls, monitoring, and supervision on the residential campus and a resultant increase in the personal freedom to engage in lifestyle choices and behaviors that may be unhealthy and self-destructive.
- An increase in substance abuse and especially in binge drinking, with such consequences as a rise in the number of students who drive while under the influence.[3]
- A lack of peer censure for obvious intoxication and its related (formerly unacceptable) behaviors.
- An increase in the abuse of prescription drugs, especially prescription stimulants (usually prescribed for attention deficit disorder) and prescription opiates.
- An increase in psychologically and physically abusive relationships.
- The abuse of technology to monitor, control, stalk, and harass peers and to invade their privacy.
- The ever-increasing cost of a college education, coupled with financial crises, unemployment, and a slowing national economy, in general.
- Increasing anxiety about such issues as finding employment, violent incidents on the campus, terrorism, and concerns about being able to manage the demands of adult life.[4]

Perhaps these factors account for statistics that you as a parent should be aware of. In October 2009, 70 percent of youth age 16–24 in the United States (who had graduated from high school between January and October, 2009) were enrolled in college; 60 percent were enrolled at four-year institutions. This is a positive finding until one reviews the actual recent rates of college completion by undergraduate students. For example, only 45 percent of recent high school graduates completed a bachelor's degree in six years, according to the National Center for Education Statistics at the U.S. Department of Education.[5]

We offer this last statistic and present some of the challenges that might account for it, not to frighten you. Rather, our purpose is to inform you about some of the realities of college life in order to empower you, as a parent, with information that will help you assist your child in his or her persistence to graduation.

You should be aware that as a parent, you have a critical role to play in this regard. A recent survey of college students indicated that 67 percent reported that they would turn to parents for help when they experienced stress or suicidal thoughts (as compared to 29 percent who would turn to a school counselor).[6] This is not to suggest in any way that you are expected to respond as a trained mental health provider. However, because your student is likely to turn to you for assistance, knowing how to effectively respond to your son or daughter in crisis is of paramount importance.

The purpose of this book is to help you do exactly that, as well as to guide your son or daughter through the more normal, developmental transitions to college life.

Specifically, in this book we will help you to

- Assist your son or daughter in making a wise decision about college selection
- Recognize the warning signs and risk factors for psychological distress
- Know when and how to intervene appropriately to access help for your college student
- Know about the protective factors and strategies that work to enhance your student's potential for academic success and emotional wellness
- Be aware of the normal developmental and transitional aspects of starting college, as well as those that are more serious and require your assistance
- Find the balance between being supportive and caring, versus being intrusive and unhelpful, to your student's growing maturity and autonomy[7]
- Be aware of the resources, programs, and student services available on the campus that can help your student negotiate the complex and challenging collegiate environment successfully

We know that, as a parent, you want your son or daughter to have the best, happiest, and most successful college experience possible. In this book, we will provide the in-depth information you need, as well as the strategies you can use, to effectively assist your student in getting the most out of his or her college years. We want to note that for the sake of simplicity, we use the term *parent* throughout this book; however, this term is meant to also include legal guardians, grandparents, and other significant caregivers.

WHO CAN BENEFIT FROM THIS BOOK?

Although parents and other significant caregivers are our primary audience, additional cohorts will find this book useful. For example, parents and students frequently turn to high school counselors and educators for advice and assistance with the college selection and admissions process.

Therefore, high school counselors and teachers will find this book to be a helpful resource with regard to guiding parents and students through the confusing maze of factors that go into finding a campus that is a good fit. This book also provides high school counselors and teachers with a clear and realistic picture of the challenges that students will face as they transition from high school to college life. This information will be useful for counselors who wish to offer psychoeducational programs that will ease the transition for their graduating seniors and better prepare them for campus life.

College and university faculty will also find this book useful for a number of reasons. On the most basic level, faculty will gain considerable insight into what their students may be experiencing outside of the classroom that, nevertheless, may significantly affect their performance in the classroom. Also, increasingly, on many campuses, faculty are asked to be aware of signs and symptoms of at-risk students who may pose a danger to themselves or to other members of the community.

On the one hand, this expectation is reasonable in that faculty have more ongoing contact with students than any other group of campus professionals. They are therefore in the best position to observe student behavior and to note whether the behavior of a particular student is deteriorating. On the other hand, members of the faculty are, for the most part, not trained mental health professionals, and they may therefore feel uncomfortable with the task of taking note of behavior that may suggest psychological impairment.

This book offers in-depth discussions of psychological disorders that are particularly relevant to a college-student population, including warning signs that faculty would be able to recognize in the classroom. This book also includes a discussion of mental health and other resources for students that are available on the campus, as well as suggestions for how to refer students to these services. In sum, the faculty member who is committed to educating "the whole student" will find this book to be eye opening and extremely useful in identifying and accessing help for an at-risk student.

In addition to faculty, other academic affairs and student affairs professionals are also increasingly expected to be informed about how to recognize and intervene with students of concern. Currently, in higher education, keeping the campus as safe as possible is viewed as a shared responsibility among all members of the community, particularly professional staff.

College and university mental health care providers, including social workers, mental health counselors, and psychologists, are increasingly called upon to provide orientation and other psychoeducational programs for the parents and other caregivers of college students. This book will provide a wealth of information that mental health providers can draw upon in order to create effective and useful programs for parents.

In sum, parents, high school counselors and teachers, college and university faculty, and other campus professionals and campus mental health providers will find a wealth of useful information in this book.

BRIEF OVERVIEW BY CHAPTER

In chapter 1, we will present an overall model and framework for relating to your college student. We also discuss such issues as privacy, expectations for the college student, and relevant cultural issues within the parent-child relationship. Finally, we will set out recommendations for when it is most appropriate to coach from the sidelines and when it is important to directly intervene when your child is in distress.

Chapter 2 will be particularly useful to the parents of a high school senior or of a student who plans to transfer to another college or university. In this chapter, we give parents the information they need to help their son or daughter select the campus that is the best possible fit for him or her. Finding an excellent fit between the student and the institution is an effective way to promote success and emotional wellness in your child right from the start. We include a discussion of what we consider to be the most salient factors in the often complex and confusing selection process. We also highlight the importance of the on-campus visit and present a comprehensive list of questions that parents and students might ask during their visit. Finally, we ask parents to candidly assess their child's readiness for college, and we offer recommendations for the continuity of care for students already in treatment for psychological issues.

In chapter 3, parents will learn about some of the issues that arise during the transition to college and what they can do to assist their student in this process. Some of the challenges that first-year students typically encounter are related to academic demands, separating from home, choosing a major, living with roommates, and negotiating differences. All of these challenges intersect with the complex process of identity development, which typically takes place during late adolescence and young adult life. For some students, there may be problems at home (for example, illness of a family member, divorce, death, unemployment), which certainly impact the student's ease of entering college. In addition, the critical significance of the first year of college will be discussed, and specific recommendations for how parents can promote their student's engagement and involvement will be offered.

In chapter 4, parents will be acquainted with some of the untoward situations that can arise on the college campus. Certainly, not all students will be affected or caught up in these situations; nevertheless, parents should be aware of these realities of today's campus life. Some of the situations we will discuss include the increase in mental health concerns, the use and abuse of alcohol and other drugs, sexual assault, unhealthy relationships, sexual harassment, roommate conflict, bullying, cyberbullying, and other issues related to the abuse of technology and cyberspace. Though relatively infrequent occurrences, bias incidents and violence on the campus will also be addressed. With each of these issues, parents will be apprised of specific actions they can engage in to prevent their child from being in some of these situations, and how they can assist their student in the event that they do experience an untoward incident.

Chapter 5 will inform parents about some of the psychological disorders observed in college students. These include depression, trauma, anger and aggression, stress and anxiety, schizophrenia, bipolar disorder, eating disorders, and the potential for dangerous behavior. Parents will also learn about chemical dependency involving such substances as alcohol, prescription drugs, and illegal drugs. The topic of addiction to gambling and to online gaming will also be presented. Parents will be assisted in recognizing the clear signs of psychological disorders and of chemical dependency and addictive behaviors. For each of these topics, parents will receive clear recommendations as to how to best assist their son or daughter.

Chapter 6 will provide parents with an in-depth picture of some of the significant campus services and resources that are available to help their college student through the normal transitional issues, as well as with more serious problems and concerns. Some of the services and resources delineated in this chapter are the counseling center/psychological services (CAPS), the office of student retention/student success, health services, alcohol and other drug services, office of residential life, office of disabilities/learning needs, office of multicultural affairs, academic resources services, career services, office of student affairs/student life, and campus safety and security. Parents will also learn about how to make referrals to student services and how they can learn even more about the resources available on campus.

In chapter 7, parents will be acquainted with some specific approaches and strategies that have been shown to be effective with regard to promoting emotional wellness and student success. These approaches include effective communication between parent and student, reducing stress and developing coping strategies, maintaining perspective, cultivating happiness, increasing self-esteem and self-respect, and encouraging healthy lifestyle choices. Parents will also be informed about the specific factors that have been shown to support success among college students and will be encouraged to become advocates for mental health and other student services on the campus.

The conclusion of this book will offer a review of the many positive aspects of college attendance and completion. It will also highlight some of the negative aspects of college life of which parents (as well as counselors, educators, and campus professionals) should be aware. Finally, the significant role of parents in enhancing the success and emotional well-being of their college student is reviewed.

Chapter One

The Role of the Parent in Promoting Emotional Wellness

A Basic Framework

It is impossible to overstate the significance of parents in promoting success and emotional wellness in their children. In the life of a young person, there can be no more powerful and enduring role model or source of influence, nurturance, and guidance than a parent. In the current generation, perhaps more than ever, young people increasingly turn to their parents for assistance and reassurance in times of trouble and for praise and positive reinforcement when times are good.

As a parent, you want to be there for your son or daughter as a consistent anchor, problem solver, comforter, and wise counselor. At the same time, you want to support your college student's growing maturity, autonomy, and sense of confidence. Balancing your role as a caring parent with promoting your child's independence and self-sufficiency can, therefore, be confusing at times.

In this chapter, parents will be introduced to a basic framework that will help distinguish between those situations that students should be encouraged to manage on their own and those that require parental intervention. The concept of the caring versus the helicopter parent will be discussed, and expectations for the student during his or her college years will be delineated. In addition, rights to privacy will be presented, as well as a discussion of how the parent-child relationship will evolve over the college years. Finally, cultural differences regarding expectations for parent-child roles and interactions will be acknowledged and explored.

ROOTS AND WINGS

There is a proverb that states, "Children need two gifts from their parents: the gift of roots and the gift of wings." There is no more important factor in the development and promotion of emotional wellness than the quality of the parent-child relationship. This most significant of all relationships provides a model for healthy relating later in life; it teaches your child to expect respectful, kind, and nurturing behavior from others, and to display those behaviors in turn. Further, the home environment that parents provide for their children, preferably one of safety, good communication, appropriate boundaries, and an absence of extensive conflict, provides a solid foundation that grounds the child securely to home and family.

Much of the first eighteen years of your child's life, therefore, has been devoted to giving him or her the gift of roots. Ideally, your child is securely attached to you and other family members, views you as a source of comfort and guidance, and views home as a safe place, at times as a haven from the stress of the outside world. But now, as your child is entering college, the gift of wings becomes equally important—giving your permission to your son or daughter to soar beyond the safety of home, to separate, to make mistakes, to handle adversity, and to move toward the independence and autonomy of emerging adulthood.

To provide both roots and wings, parents need to find the right balance between knowing when to intervene and when to let go, a distinction we will discuss in the next section.

THE CARING AND SUPPORTIVE PARENT VERSUS THE HELICOPTER PARENT

Many parents of students currently attending college have had the experience of being intimately, continuously, and minutely in touch with the academic, personal, and social lives of their children. In turn, the current college student population, known as the "Millennium Generation" or the "Millennials" (born between 1985 and 2005), has been characteristically noted for their considerable reliance on their parents.[1] Facilitated by social networking sites, cell phones, and other technologies, it is not uncommon for parents to monitor the moment-by-moment lives of their children. Actions such as text messaging, instant messaging, and monitoring Facebook accounts have given parents heretofore unparalleled access to both the public and very private lives of their children.

Understandably, this access has led, in some cases, to a blurring of boundaries between what parents have a right and a responsibility to know about their children, and what is legitimately personal information that the child has a right to regard as private. Problems can arise in the parent-child relationship when the child comes to believe that his or her privacy has been violated. Trust between parent and child can be damaged, and the child's sense of personal rights and prerogatives as a valued, but separate, human being can be harmed.

Further, because parents can have so much access to the details of their children's lives, including their interactions with peers and their moment-to-moment problems and concerns, parents may be tempted to become directly involved, regardless of whether that is appropriate or in the child's best interest. The term "helicopter parent" has been coined to describe the parent who is viewed as hovering (in helicopter fashion) too closely and sometimes inappropriately over the life of their child, particularly once he or she has entered college. This admittedly pejorative label denotes parents who are seen as crossing the line between being supportive and being intrusive. Though undoubtedly loving and well intentioned, helicopter parents may inadvertently hinder the process of their children achieving personal responsibility.[2]

These are the parents who

- provide wake-up calls every morning to make sure their child gets up for class
- step into the middle of their child's roommate conflicts
- demand that a roommate whom their child doesn't like be removed from the dorm room
- demand that college administrators immediately step in and solve their child's problem
- insist upon special considerations for their child, even if it violates campus policies and protocols
- regularly drop in for surprise visits with their child
- refuse to allow their child to suffer negative consequences
- demand to know information that is confidential or privileged about their child
- directly contact faculty to challenge their child's grade

Historically, college students have been considered to be adults within institutions of higher education, with considerable rights to privacy and explicit expectations for personal responsibility, self-regulation, and autonomous functioning. The college years have been viewed as an opportunity for students to successfully move from the life stage of late adolescence into that of being a young, or emerging, adult. The college years have been regarded as the time when students can become more separate from parents and thereby handle personal challenges, academic demands, financial concerns, and other difficulties, more and more autonomously. The helicopter parent phenomenon describes a relatively new dynamic between the parent and the college-age student, as well as between the parent and the institution.

Of course, it is perfectly understandable that, as a parent, you want to protect your child from adversity, disappointment, and negative consequences. At earlier times in your child's life, that may have been very appropriate and even necessary. Similarly, closely monitoring your child as he or she grew from infancy into early childhood and adolescence was clearly your responsibility as a parent. However, continuing to protect, monitor, and, yes, to hover may not be in your child's best interest as he or she transitions into young adult life.

That being said, we also wish to acknowledge potentially significant cultural differences with regard to the extent of expected parental involvement with their college-age child. Moving away from parental supervision and monitoring, while moving toward greater separation and autonomy, is an admittedly Western and, in fact, a mainstream American construct. Further, we recognize that within some first-generation families and some cultural and religious groups, maintaining close familial ties and strong parental influence is considered the healthy norm. We therefore invite parents who are members of these groups to filter some of the discussions in this book through their own cultural worldviews. We also ask parents to read this book with an eye toward learning about the culture of separation and individuation that is the predominant philosophy on the American college campus.

EXPECTATIONS FOR THE COLLEGE STUDENT

The academic, developmental, and interpersonal tasks that your child faces are formidable. Ideally, during their college years, students will learn how to

- develop and solidify their identity as an individual, separate person
- structure and manage their time
- set priorities and manage competing ones
- negotiate interpersonal conflicts
- make friends and create new social networks
- choose a major and make career decisions
- become competent and successful learners
- develop cocurricular interests
- manage their finances
- make healthy lifestyle choices
- solidify personal core values and spiritual beliefs
- continue their character development—that is, a sense of personal integrity, ethicality, and justice

- develop resilience and tools for coping with adversity and personal problems
- develop a healthy sense of perspective and optimism

Succeeding at these often challenging and daunting tasks requires the care and support of parents, albeit with less direct intervention than previously. Supportive and caring parents listen attentively, offer guidance when needed, and assist their son and daughter in accessing his or her own internal resources for handling difficult situations. These parents point their child to on-campus services that can help, and they express confidence in their child's ability to cope, to persevere, and to succeed.

A WORD ABOUT PRIVACY AND CONFIDENTIALITY

As part of being considered an adult on the campus, college students have both legal and ethical rights to privacy and confidentiality. Under the Family Educational Rights and Privacy Act (FERPA), the right to inspect, review, correct, and/or release educational records (which include academic, disciplinary, and financial records) passes from the parent to "eligible students," when students reach age eighteen or attend a school beyond the high school level.[3]

Under FERPA, parents may have access to educational records if their student is a financial dependent, and they may have a right to be notified regarding disciplinary actions taken related to their student violating the alcohol or other drug policy at their institution. However, colleges and universities are not *required* to provide notification regarding disciplinary actions, and some states have passed regulations that prohibit these disclosures. Parents who would like to learn more about FERPA may visit the website of the U.S. Department of Education at http://www.2.ed.gov/policy/gen/guid/fpco/ferpa/.

In addition, under the Health Insurance Portability and Accountability Act (HIPAA), the legal right to privacy regarding physical and mental health medical records passes from the parent to the child at age eighteen.[4] Generally, college and university health services and counseling centers are required to be HIPAA compliant. However, even when counseling centers do not fall under mandatory HIPAA regulation, they often comply voluntarily. Further, all counseling centers must abide by state laws and codes of ethics with regard to confidentiality and privacy.

In sum, then, student records regarding grades, disciplinary actions, finances, and/or visits to health or counseling services on the campus are generally protected and can be released only with the student's permission. As a parent, you may understandably be dismayed to learn that your access to your child's records may be limited or even curtailed upon his or her turning eighteen or starting college. However, parents are encouraged to view the right to safeguard private information as a significant marker on the path of transitioning from the life stage of adolescence to that of emerging adulthood.

Parents will be comforted to know that, given healthy communication within the family, many students voluntarily disclose information regarding grades, medical concerns, and psychological issues to their parents. Certainly, parents have every right to communicate their expectations to their children regarding information that they would like to receive about their overall functioning at college—for example, how they are doing academically, whether they are attending classes, and whether anything is troubling them. Parents should also know that, in times of crisis, mental health care providers often encourage students to put their parents in the loop, and in situations of imminent danger, mental health providers *can* breach confidentiality and inform parents. In addition, FERPA does not preclude other college employees, such as faculty or administrators, from discussing their serious concerns about a student's welfare with his or her parents or with other college personnel, as appropriate.

KNOWING WHEN TO LET GO

Imagine that your child calls you in a panic and tells you that her roommates are completely excluding her, that her teachers are being ridiculous, that they all think their class is the only one she is taking, and that she is missing you terribly and wants to come home—*now*! Phone calls like this understandably tug at the heartstrings of parents, and the impulse to rush in and make it all better immediately is almost universal. How then to resist the urge to fix it, to intervene, to anxiously hover? How can you begin to let go, even when your child is expressing distress?

Here are some recommendations we would like to offer:

- Ask yourself whether this is a genuine crisis that demands your immediate intervention or a situation that your child is capable of handling, perhaps with some coaching from you on the sidelines.
- Ask yourself whether it is in your child's best interest for you to rescue him or her from every uncomfortable situation.
- Remind yourself that loosening the reins is not abandoning your child. You will still be there as an anchor in really difficult times.
- Consider the long-range consequences of your child's not developing the skills he or she needs to handle uncomfortable feelings, resolve conflict, cope with adversity, accept consequences, and solve problems.

- Get the support you need to manage your own fears and apprehensions about letting go.[5]

YOUR CHANGING RELATIONSHIP WITH YOUR CHILD

When a child goes off to college, it can be a bittersweet time for parents. On the one hand, you are rightfully bursting with pride that your son or daughter has reached this significant milestone. At the same time, it is natural to experience sadness at your child's departure from home. You may be worried about your child's adjustment to college and living on his or her own. You may be concerned about how your child will do academically and how he or she will cope without your reassuring presence.

A common fear is that of "losing" your child as he or she becomes more separate and self-sufficient. In fact, nothing can be further from the truth. Your child needs your love, approval, and support now more than ever. Your child needs to know that as he or she grows, changes, and becomes independent, your love remains unconditional. Your child also needs to know that if he or she makes mistakes, makes some bad decisions, and yes, experiences some failures, your confidence in your child remains steadfast. Over the course of your son's or daughter's journey through college, as he or she leaves adolescence behind and moves toward the next stage of life, your child will deeply value your affirmation of the adult he or she is becoming.

In fact, your child's growth toward greater maturity, increasing self-reflection, exploration of values, and growing curiosity about the world may well deepen your bond with him or her. You will experience the gratification of talking to your son or daughter on an adult-to-adult level. You will marvel at how facile his or her mind is, and you will experience great pleasure in listening to the ever-increasing complexity of his or her thoughts and personal musings.

By providing the bedrock security of roots, and by also giving your child the gift of wings, you have created the space in which he or she can expand and excitedly embrace both the freedoms and responsibilities of adult life. You have nurtured an emotionally healthy individual, and you have created the possibility of enjoying a mature, genuinely adult relationship with your son or daughter.

WHEN SHOULD A PARENT GET INVOLVED?

Throughout this chapter, parents have been advised to maintain a stance of encouragement and support when their child encounters challenges, without jumping in to solve the problem. Parents have been admonished to refrain from being intrusive and quickly becoming involved. For the most part, maintaining a respectful distance and allowing their child to struggle with and overcome challenges promotes emotional wellness by building resilience and a sense of competence.

However, at times it is appropriate, and even necessary, for parents to decisively intervene in their children's lives. When your son or daughter is not simply struggling with the unpleasant but to-be-expected challenges of college life, but is seriously floundering and becoming hopeless about ever turning things around, parents must get involved. If your son or daughter has experienced an assault, is in an abusive relationship, has been targeted in a bias incident, has been bullied or harassed, parents should actively assist and protect him or her. Most significantly, if your child is displaying symptoms of addiction, self-injurious behavior, or other mental disorders, it is imperative that you as a parent intervene in order to access appropriate professional help for your child. College students who find themselves in traumatic situations or who are becoming psychologically impaired cannot reasonably be expected to manage these circumstances on their own.

If these issues are of current concern to you, please consult chapter 4 to learn about some of the more serious problems your child might encounter on the college campus, or chapter 5 to learn about the signs and symptoms of mental disorders and addiction. Chapter 6 will provide you with information about the services that are available to your child on campus.

Chapter 2 will be most useful to parents of high school students (and their counselors and faculty) and to parents whose students are considering a transfer to another campus. Helping your son or daughter choose a college that is the best possible fit for him or her will go a long way toward promoting your child's emotional well-being and success on the campus. In addition, it will assist you in making a determination about whether your child is actually ready to leave home and enter college. It will also address concerns you might have if your child has already experienced serious emotional and psychological problems.

Chapter Two

Helping Your Child with College Selection and Preparation

The process of assisting your son or daughter in selecting the college that is right for him or her is a complex, often confusing, and overwhelming task. What factors should be most important to consider: academic reputation, rankings in such publications as *U.S. News and World Report*, cocurricular activities, the "feel" of the campus? Are there other factors to consider as well? How do you prioritize the myriad considerations that go into making a decision of this magnitude?

In this chapter, parents will be advised to consider a number of factors, such as finances, academic reputation, curriculum, retention and graduation rates, culture, faculty contact, and availability of student services, in assisting their child in finding the best collegiate fit for her or him. Parents will also be challenged to reflect on whether their child is ready to leave home for college and to consider other options to ease the transition for their child.

This chapter will also be especially useful for high school counselors and teachers. Parents often turn to these professionals for assistance with navigating the complex maze of college selection. As a high school counselor or faculty member, you will find this chapter to be invaluable in assisting parents and students in becoming aware of significant variables they should consider and prioritize in their selection process. This chapter will also include many resources for parents, online and on-campus, with which you can acquaint them. Further, it will present an extensive list of questions that parents and students might pose to make the most of their on-campus visit.

Perhaps most importantly, you are the high school professionals who are the most likely to have significant insights about your students' level of academic functioning, maturity, conduct, self-control, and social skills. As such, you are the most reliable and valuable sources of information that parents need to make the very difficult decision of whether their son or daughter is actually academically, psychologically, and interpersonally ready to enter college and to function successfully and responsibly in that setting.

THE IMPORTANCE OF THE BEST FIT

Simply put, the answer to how to navigate the complex maze of college selection lies in guiding your child to find the best possible fit for him or her. This involves, first and foremost, your thoroughly knowing your child and helping him or her to be clear about what kind of learning environment, curriculum, campus atmosphere, peer group, and cocurricular activities best suit him or her.

If your son or daughter is a nonconforming, artistic, highly individualistic young person who "marches to a different drum," a college in which most students are focused on their institution's varsity athletics program, tend to join a fraternity or sorority, and embrace a "preppy" persona will not be a good fit for your child.

If he or she needs a great deal of individual attention from teachers, works best in small groups, and tends to get lost and fall through the cracks in large, crowded environments, a large state university, though often an excellent choice financially, may not work for your son or daughter. Similarly, if your child has already struggled with emotional problems, learning challenges, shyness, and fitting in, a smaller campus may offer a better environment in which your child can grow and develop.

Clearly the most significant way to promote children's success and emotional well-being on the campus is to help them honestly reflect upon who they really are and what they need to succeed. It is also important to urge them to thoroughly investigate the colleges they are seriously considering. It is not uncommon for high school seniors to become overwhelmed by the college selection process and to withdraw from it or make a hasty, ill-considered choice, just to bring closure to a difficult process. However, this is virtually always an error. Similarly, we are surprised by the number of students who select a college without visiting the campus. This is perhaps the most serious mistake that students and parents can make in the process of selecting a college.

As with other important life decisions, often the most difficult part is getting started. Parents can assist their daughters and sons to begin this challenging process by:

- Initiating the process of college selection early enough to allow ample time to thoroughly investigate a number of schools, to make a number of on-campus visits, and to carefully consider a number of viable options.

- Engaging your son or daughter in conversations about what their ideal college experience would be like: What would they like to study? Who would their friends be? What would the campus atmosphere be like? How would they like to socialize? What kinds of student activities, clubs, or organizations might they want to get involved in? If they already have well-developed interests and activities, can they pursue them in the schools they are considering?
- Sharing what your college experience was like for you, both positively and negatively. This is an area in which your child can very much benefit from your experience.
- Encouraging your child to make the best possible use of his or her high school counselor. The counselor can help your child identify a manageable and realistic subgroup of colleges and universities to which to apply. Counselors designated to offer assistance to college-bound students have expertise in matching students' academic record, special skills and needs, and personality to institutions that are a good fit for them. The assistance of the high school counselor in narrowing an overwhelming number of possibilities to a group that is manageable, and in selecting institutions where admission is attainable for your child, should be utilized to the fullest extent possible.
- Helping your child to be patient, to maintain perspective, to manage anxiety and frustration, and to understand that this is a process that will take time, but is well worth it.
- Exploring resources for current and future parents of college students that orient you to the application and admissions process and thereafter, such as College Parents of America (http://www.collegeparents.org) and publications by the College Board (http://www.collegeboard.com).
- Encouraging your child to consult with members of the high school faculty, particularly in areas of study that he or she might be inclined to pursue on the campus. Faculty members are invaluable sources of information about which colleges and universities offer especially good programs in areas of interest for your child. They may recommend their own alma mater, if appropriate, or other institutions about which they have extensive information.
- Making your child aware that high school teachers can help him or her connect with faculty in higher education who they believe to be excellent and reliable sources of information about their field of study. High school faculty thus can mentor your son or daughter through college selection, and in some cases open doors and provide direct access on a given campus that your child would not otherwise have.
- Also making your child aware that, in addition to providing mentorship, introductions, and connections, high school faculty can be sources of encouragement and empowerment for your child. Because high school facul-

ty are intimately aware of your child's academic performance, they can credibly tell your child, "I know that you can do this. You are absolutely capable of being successful in this program."

SOME FACTORS TO CONSIDER

Academic Reputation and Rankings

Understandably, colleges and universities that are prestigious and well known for their academic reputation are extremely attractive to parents and prospective students. Often, more prestigious institutions of higher education also emerge at the top of college ranking systems, such as the one conducted by *U.S. News and World Report*. This and other ranking systems include such relevant key indicators as freshman to sophomore retention rate, six-year graduation rate, percentage of classes with fifty or less students, student-faculty ratio, acceptance rate, high school class rank of admitted students, and percentage of full-time faculty.

However, the ranking process may also contain such variables as alumni giving rate and faculty resources, which may or may not be relevant to overall student satisfaction with the institution or to resources available for students. Parents and prospective students can view results on key indicators for colleges of interest by accessing the *U.S. News and World Report* website (http://www.colleges.usnews.rankingandreviews.com).

Retention and Graduation Rates

Although academic reputation and national rankings certainly should be factors that merit serious consideration, perhaps the most salient factors to consider are whether the institution retains its students from year to year and what percentage persist through graduation. Parents are often surprised to learn that these figures vary significantly among institutions. Parents and students make enormous sacrifices in the service of attending college, with the clear and explicit goal of graduating and thereby gleaning the many concomitant financial, intellectual, and personal benefits.

Given the enormity of the financial investment, hard work, and effort that go into reaching this goal, it is imperative that parents know the track records of the institutions under consideration in successfully graduating their students within a reasonable time frame (four to six years). Freshman retention and graduation rates for colleges and universities can be found by accessing the *U.S. News and World Report* website (www.colleges.usnews.rankingsandreviews.com).

Finances

It is an incontrovertible reality that cost must be a primary concern in choosing a college. Currently, tuition and room and board run into the tens of thousands of dollars annually, with increases each year on both. In addition to these costs, parents must consider books (which tend to run into hundreds of dollars each semester), personal computers, travel, clothing, entertainment, special fees, and many incidentals. Although most college students are on financial aid, the burden on students and families remains considerable.

Parents can learn more specific information about the *actual* cost of a college education at a specific institution, and about which colleges and universities have the lowest tuition and lowest net price, by visiting the College Affordability and Transparency Center provided by the U.S. Department of Education (http://www.collegecost.ed.gov/catc/).

Some financial considerations for parents are as follows:

- Consider the amount of debt your college-bound student and your family are willing to incur in the long run.
- If your student is reasonably certain that he or she will be attending graduate, law, or medical school, factor that in as you consider the cost of undergraduate school.
- Thoroughly investigate the financial aid packages, scholarships, stipends, tuition remission opportunities, and other cost reduction possibilities available on the campus that your son or daughter is considering. This information is often available on the college's student financial services website.
- Carefully calculate how much money your son or daughter will have to contribute to cover expenses while in college. Take into account that the hours they spend in paid employment should not interfere with their successful academic performance.
- Encourage your son or daughter to look into how affluent the general student population is on a prospective campus. At a school where a substantial number of students are financially privileged, if your child is less privileged or barely getting by, she or he could feel this discrepancy keenly and painfully.
- If you are going through a divorce, make sure that financial issues regarding your child's college education have been resolved prior to college selection. Students sometimes get caught in the financial crossfire of a divorce, experiencing a great deal of anxiety over who will be paying for what during their college years.
- Consider your child starting his or her studies at a cost-effective community college. Generally these credits will transfer to a four-year school.

Some community colleges have honors programs, making it possible for successful students to transfer to first-tier institutions.
- Teach your son or daughter how to manage money *now*, by creating a budget, spending money appropriately, earning money, and living within his or her means.
- Be aware that college students are being offered opportunities to get their own credit cards. Set clear expectations about whether or not this is acceptable to you and the limits on spending you wish to impose.

Location and Distance from Home

In considering the best fit of a college or university for your daughter or son, the location and setting are key variables. If your child thrives in an urban environment and is energized and inspired by city life, an institution in a more remote rural setting will likely be unduly challenging. Therefore, although you may find a campus to be lovely and the surrounding area to be rich in natural beauty, your city girl or boy may feel isolated and dislocated in this environment. Conversely, for the young person who is outdoorsy and thrives in environments that provide open spaces to recreate, such an environment could prove ideal.

Similarly, extreme changes in climate from where the student grew up can be challenging for some. Prospective college students should realistically assess how much they are affected by weather and availability of sunlight. For students who grew up in warm, sunny climates, the change to long, cold, dreary winters can be especially daunting. Students should be realistic about what being cooped up indoors, dealing with extreme cold and snow, and limited sunlight will mean for their sense of well-being. Seasonal affective disorder (SAD) is a real phenomenon, causing depressive symptoms in the face of limited sunlight in some individuals. It is important to assess whether your child is a possible or even likely candidate for developing this problem.

Distance from home is a related factor to consider for many students. If your child needs to literally be close to home, being a car ride of not more than a few hours away would add to his or her sense of comfort and security. Some students need to know that they can readily go home for an evening or overnight, or certainly for a weekend, in order to make the transition to college. Others can be a continent away and be perfectly comfortable. Again, prospective college students should honestly and realistically evaluate where they fall on this continuum.

School Size and Class Size

In finding the best fit for your child, the overall size of the institution is an obvious but often overlooked factor. Students who crave individual attention and prefer to be "a big fish in a small pond" will likely feel lost in an enormous institution that numbers in the tens of thousands. Similarly, students already identified as having psychological concerns or learning disabilities are more likely to be referred to appropriate resources in a smaller institution. Socially, some students will be overwhelmed by large student populations, and students who crave leadership roles may find them easier to access in a smaller school.

On the other hand, some students are wary of "everyone knowing my business" in a smaller school and relish the adventure of engaging a very large, diverse student population. In addition, larger institutions may have more resources, such as a greater number of potential academic majors, fitness and recreation resources, and lavish student unions or student activity centers, as well as state-of-the-art technology. However, larger institutions often offer introductory courses in large lecture halls with hundreds of students, often taught by teaching assistants, and a paucity of actual student-to-faculty contact.

Smaller institutions, by way of contrast, often have classes with fewer than fifty students, taught by full-time faculty, and many classes are offered with even smaller enrollments. Prospective students should carefully self-assess how class size will affect their academic performance. Bear in mind that students who attended small private high schools or small schools in rural settings may feel completely overwhelmed by walking into a large lecture hall in which the number of students exceeds the entire population of their high school.

Faculty

The reputation of the faculty directly affects the overall reputation of the institution. Visible and productive researchers, Nobel Prize winners, and other high-profile faculty members clearly enhance an institution's academic prestige and reputation. However, parents should be mindful of whether these academic luminaries will actually be teaching their children. At times, these individuals do not have a teaching load, and if they do, it is at the graduate level. In fact, at some institutions, teaching assistants may offer a considerable amount of classroom instruction at the undergraduate level. Therefore, parents should investigate how much of the instruction their children will receive is actually provided by fully credentialed and experienced faculty members.

Curriculum and Academic Resources

As with other factors, course offerings and majors should be carefully investigated well in advance of enrollment. Parents may be surprised to learn how often students enroll in college only to find that their choice of a major is not offered on their campus or is offered as a minor. Also, such courses as ethnic studies, feminist studies, and extensive selections in specific diverse populations, in the performing and visual arts, and in nursing, physical therapy, or other potential careers are not offered on all campuses. Therefore, carefully scrutinizing the college catalog prior to application is a must. Prospective students should thoroughly investigate whether all of their possible choices of majors and other subjects that they are interested in pursuing are offered on the campus.

An additional factor to consider is whether there is an honors program for academically gifted and talented students. Honors programs often offer a more sophisticated and intellectually complex array of courses, interdisciplinary courses and instruction, a waiver of prerequisite courses, and other academic advantages. With regard to academic resources, the campus library is a key factor. Indicators of an excellent library facility are technological sophistication; access to an extensive enough array of books, periodicals, and professional journals for students to readily complete all research projects; and availability of professional staff to assist students.

Student Population and Diversity Resources

One of the most important factors in the best-fit evaluation is who your child's peers will be. Looking at the overall culture of the campus (sporty? artsy? preppy? traditional? politically active? service oriented? multicultural?) is a first step in helping prospective students to determine whether they will fit in.

Equally important for a racial minority or biracial student, an LGBT student, an international, first-generation, or religious minority student is the availability of resources and student organizations that will support him or her. It is important for ensuring that your son or daughter is entering a hospitable campus environment to investigate whether there are such organizations as an LGBT alliance; black, Hispanic, Asian, African descent, South Asian, and/or Middle Eastern student organizations; academic clubs for women and visible minority students; and an office for multicultural affairs. It is also important to investigate whether the composition of the faculty and administration mirrors that of the student population, so that culturally appropriate mentors and role models are available on the campus.

For students who are interested in fraternity/sorority organizations, investigating what proportion of the student population is involved on the campus is relevant. For the "sports nut," the level of engagement of the institution in Division I varsity competition and the scope of its intramural program may greatly enhance that student's college experience. Similarly, if your son or daughter has been active in the performing arts, an investigation into these opportunities on the campus will be important.

The student who has been involved in volunteer and service activities in high school should be aware of whether this is an important aspect of college life on their prospective campus. The student who is religious and deeply spiritual should ascertain whether there are organizations and resources on the campus that will support and nurture this aspect of his or her growth and development. In sum, students being readily able to connect with affinity groups, continuing those activities that they find especially rewarding in high school, and accessing mentors and cultural resources will be critical in their feeling at home on the campus.

Housing Options

For students planning to live away from home, exploring the array of on-campus and off-campus living options is important. As with other factors we have explored, on-campus housing options may vary significantly among campuses. For example, residential life opportunities may offer apartment-style living, single rooms, ten-person suites, multiple occupancy rooms, traditional residence halls, actual apartments in nearby buildings, or even hotel rooms in nearby facilities. Further, campuses vary in the availability of on-campus living facilities.

Students who want the safety and convenience of living on campus for all of their undergraduate career should be aware that not all campuses offer this option. Students who wish to live off-campus, or who must move off-campus in their junior or senior year, should investigate whether there is an off-campus housing office to offer assistance with finding safe, affordable housing.

Within the options available in residential life facilities, there is also considerable variation in special options such as wellness or substance-free floors; quiet floors; and housing by cohorts such as honors students, athletes, international students, LGBT students, and others. Some on-campus options include living/learning communities that invite faculty and administrators to live in the residence hall in order to offer programs, seminars, and contact on a regular basis.

Students with special needs should certainly investigate whether their needs can be met within student housing. For example, it is important to know whether all residence halls and facilities are accessible and whether "psychological singles" are available for students who cannot share a living space (for such reasons as panic disorder, Asperger's or other autism spectrum disorders, or social phobia). A student's dorm room or apartment will be his or her home for the next four years. It should be as physically, psychologically, and interpersonally comfortable as possible in order to support the student's success and wellness on the campus.

Services for Special Needs Students

As with other factors to consider, colleges vary with regard to the depth and breadth of services available to students with physical and/or learning disabilities. Some colleges and universities offer extensive, wraparound services, including individual tutoring and academic coaching available multiple times a week; individual and group counseling; and other forms of academic, psychological, and social support. All colleges should have an accommodations compliance office that ensures that the institution is in full compliance with accommodations provided for in the Americans with Disabilities Act Amendments Act (ADAAA) of 2008.

Parents should be aware that not all campuses offer complete and extensive services to special needs students. Some will meet the minimum requirements under the law and offer little beyond what is legally required. Parents should also be aware that at some institutions, not all areas of the campus are necessarily physically accessible. For students for whom physical accessibility is critical, it will be very discouraging and frustrating to find out after enrollment that there will be limitations on where they can take classes, the extent to which they can participate in cocurricular activities and recreation, or where they can live. Therefore, parents and prospective students are urged to meticulously investigate exactly what services, resources, and programs are easily accessible on their prospective campus.

Cocurricular Activities and Student Services

A factor of paramount importance in the retention of first-year students is called "engagement," a measure of how actively students are involved in their college education experience, inside and outside of the classroom. In fact, research has found that students who do not interact with peers and other college constituencies outside of the classroom are less satisfied with their college experience and more likely to drop out.[1]

Therefore, cocurricular activities such as becoming involved in clubs and organizations, being active in student governance and on-campus media, seeking leadership positions, and attending social and cultural events are very important for student retention and persistence to graduation. Students and parents can easily learn about the range of student activities, clubs, and organizations available on a prospective campus by visiting the campus life, student affairs, student development, or student activities website.

In addition, more than six hundred colleges and universities participate in the National Survey of Student Engagement (NSSE) each year, which investigates the myriad variables that comprise student engagement on a given campus. Parents can learn more about this program and whether a prospective institution is a participant by visiting the NSSE website (http://www.nsse.iub.edu).

An equally critical outside-of-the-classroom indicator and predictor of student success is the availability of student services, such as personal and psychological counseling services, career development office, academic tutoring and coaching, health services, office for special needs accommodations/ADAAA compliance, retention office, cross-cultural affairs, campus ministries, and the office of alcohol and other drug education.

At one time or another, over their four years in school, most if not all students will access some of these services in order to be successful and well. Each of those services support and enhance the educational mission of the institution by helping students ameliorate internal and external barriers to their success. For the parent of a prospective college student, a visit to the institution's student services website should offer a quick snapshot of the availability of these critical resources on the campus. Student services will be more completely delineated and discussed fully in chapter 6 of this book.

Structured First-Year Experience

Colleges vary greatly with regard to what they offer to first-year students by way of a structured, extended orientation-to-college experience. By far, the most effective program is the first-year seminar, which is an actual course that extends over several meetings and often for a full semester. Ideally, the first-year seminar includes topics relevant to enhancing academic skills; learning about physical, emotional, and interpersonal wellness; and beginning the process of choosing a major and a possible career path.

First-year seminars also encourage and facilitate student engagement by educating participants about the resources and cocurricular offerings on their campus. Some first-year seminars teach students about the unique history, legacy, and traditions of their institution, thereby making them feel more intimately connected to their campus. First-year seminars also encourage bonding among students and with the instructor, facilitating both a cohesive peer cohort and the connection to a mentor.

Some institutions offer the first-year seminar for college credit, making them even more attractive options for students. However, students should be encouraged to participate regardless of whether the seminar is credit bearing, because participation will significantly facilitate their successful transition to college. Not surprisingly, research has shown consistently that structured first-year experiences are positively related to student engagement, retention, and persistence to graduation.[2]

Some institutions, while not offering a formal first-year seminar, may provide another type of extended first-year experience. Examples may include grouping freshman courses together in student cohorts, multiple meetings with specially selected freshmen advisers, a series of mandatory workshops, and/or structured orientation programs for all first-year students. Parents are advised to fully investigate exactly what kind of first-year experience a prospective college will offer to their son or daughter. The quality of this program may be viewed as a key indicator of how committed the institution is to facilitating student success and retention.

THE ON-CAMPUS VISIT

Arguably the most important step in the complex college selection process is the on-campus visit. Ultimately, this is the best way a prospective college student can make an informed decision about whether the institution is a good fit for him or her. Too often, students select a college based on information they read and see on the website, which they take at face value, only to be profoundly disappointed upon their arrival on the campus. At times, students do select a college for very solid reasons, only to find out after they have enrolled that the campus is far more isolated than they imagined or that they absolutely do not fit in with their peers or the culture of the institution.

The pain and misery experienced by entering students upon realizing that they have made a serious mistake in their selection process is heartbreaking to witness. It is also entirely preventable by taking the time to make an on-campus visit prior to enrolling at a college or university.

Parents who are concerned about the cost involved in visiting multiple campuses should be aware that this is a bargain when compared to the money lost when a student withdraws from school. Often tuition for that semester is not refundable after a certain point early in the academic year, and students may be liable for a full year of room and board. (Tuition and housing contracts should therefore be carefully reviewed prior to enrollment.)

The on-campus visit will allow the prospective student to interact with currently enrolled students; to extensively tour the campus; to actually see its location, its facilities, and resources; and to sit in on classes, visit the residence halls, and absorb the overall atmosphere and "feel" of the campus. Both prospective students and parents can ask any and every question they have about academics, resources, campus life, financial aid, cocurricular activities, and anything else that is of interest to them.

Parents can help their prospective college students prepare for the on-campus visit by strongly encouraging them to do their homework ahead of time. Prior to their visit, prospective students and parents should learn as much as they can about those aspects of the institution that are important to them. Although parents should be thoroughly prepared, they should also bear in mind that their son or daughter will ultimately have to live with the decision. Therefore, the college must be the best academic, social, and psychological fit for the student.

Both prospective students and parents are advised to prepare a list of questions prior to their visit. Some sample questions might include the following:

- Are the majors I might be interested in offered on this campus?
- Are cocurricular activities I might be interested in available on this campus? Performing arts? Volunteering for community service? Fraternity/sorority organizations? Intramural sports? Cultural organizations? Environmental concerns groups and projects? Political activism? Media? Leadership opportunities?
- Are tutoring services available to all students?
- What kinds of freshman orientation and first-year seminar experiences are available to students? Is there an orientation for parents?
- How do residents select roommates? How are roommate disputes handled? What if a resident wants a room change?
- If a student withdraws from the college, what fees is she or he liable for? Full tuition? Room and board?
- How can students readily meet peers? Become involved in student activities? Find out what's going on at the college?
- Ask current students: Are you happy here? What do you like about going to school here? Do you like your classes? Are there any problems you've encountered? What is the typical student like? What is there to do here at night and on weekends?
- What student services are available? Personal counseling? Health and wellness? Career development? Learning needs? Accommodations office? Multicultural affairs? Alcohol and other drugs services?
- How are issues related to diversity addressed on this campus?
- How does this campus create a hospitable environment for all students?
- What kinds of honors programs or other distinctive academic programs are available?
- Do the residence halls have learning communities, specially designated floors, or other distinctive programs?
- Are all areas of the campus physically accessible?
- What kinds of opportunities are there for students to interact with faculty outside of the classroom—for example, on research projects or to receive mentoring or advising?
- What kinds of internship experiences are available for students?
- What percentage of undergraduate classes are taught by full-time faculty?
- What percentage of first-year students are retained into sophomore year?

- What is the four-year graduation rate?
- What percentage of students are receiving financial aid?
- What scholarships are available? Work-study? Other on-campus employment?
- How friendly, available, and helpful are the employees at this college?
- How big a problem are drugs and alcohol on this campus? How is this problem being addressed?
- What safety precautions and procedures are in place in the event of an emergency, such as a fire, a natural disaster, or a violent situation on campus?
- If I think my son or daughter has a serious problem, how can I get help for him or her? Whom should I speak to?
- How can I find out how many and what kinds of crimes have been committed on or near the campus in the last few years?[3]

In sum, by doing good preparation for a campus visit (for example, by learning as much as possible about the institution prior to a visit and by preparing a list of questions), prospective students and their parents can get the most out of their on-campus visit. Both parents and students should come away from the visit satisfied that their questions have been answered and with a good "feel" for the institution.

For parents, the most important questions they need answered in their own minds are these: Will my child be happy here? Will my child succeed here? Will my child be cared for and supported on this campus? Will my child have the resources he or she needs to complete his or her college education at this institution?

A DIFFICULT QUESTION FOR PARENTS: IS MY CHILD READY?

Although typically in the United States the majority of entering freshmen are eighteen years old, this certainly does not mean that everyone is actually ready to start college at this age. Nevertheless, by age eighteen, your child has been bombarded by attractive, multimedia recruitment materials from many colleges and universities, has been surrounded by peers vying for entry into the country's most prestigious schools, has studied for SATs, written college essays, and even made campus visits.

School counselors, parents, peers, and college admissions offices have inadvertently conspired to put most high school juniors and seniors on a fast-moving treadmill that inevitably leads to entering college as the only logical next step after high school graduation. The treadmill then continues to move inexorably toward successful completion of college by age twenty-two, as if there were a cosmic timetable to which all young people must submit.

If all colleges and universities could report stellar retention rates for freshman to sophomore year and for persistence to graduation, the treadmill approach to all college-bound students entering immediately upon high school graduation would make sense. However, retention and four-year graduation rates are not as high as parents might expect. In fact, parents may be surprised to learn that many middle-tier institutions struggle to graduate 50 percent of their undergraduate students within four years. This reality may reasonably lead a parent to ask whether pushing everyone to start college by age eighteen is actually a good idea, or whether this is a contributing factor in disappointing retention and graduation rates.

Certainly, financial factors, such as those that pervade the national economy as well as financial setbacks that befall a particular family, contribute very significantly to college drop-out rates. In fact, this is a primary reason that students give for voluntarily leaving college. However, many college students get themselves into academic and disciplinary difficulties due to immaturity, an inability to live within boundaries, poor coping and anger management skills, poor study habits, underdeveloped basic life skills, serious emotional and psychological problems, and/or the abuse of drugs and alcohol.

As will be discussed fully in the next two chapters, college life provides much freedom and relatively little supervision, an abundance of temptations and distractions, and a paucity of external controls. Therefore, the seventeen- or eighteen-year-old who will successfully make the transition to college and will persist is one who is reasonably mature, responsible, self-disciplined, and essentially capable of taking care of himself or herself. Although many sources of help and support are available on the campus, the student has to be responsible enough to seek them out. However, no student service can overcome the challenges facing the young person who is simply not ready to be there at age seventeen or eighteen.

Some examples of issues that could negatively affect readiness to leave home at the start of college include:

- Dealing with a serious psychological problem that has involved a recent psychiatric hospitalization for such issues as a suicide attempt, unremitting clinical depression, bipolar disorder, self-injury, a psychotic episode, or danger to others
- Recent inpatient treatment for alcohol or other drug abuse
- An unresolved eating disorder such as bulimia or anorexia
- An unresolved physical disorder, such as a seizure disorder that is not adequately controlled by medication
- A psychological problem that requires intensive treatment and monitoring by a therapist and a psychiatrist
- Ongoing problems with anger and conduct

- Ongoing problems with social anxiety or phobia, isolation, or extreme difficulty connecting with peers
- General immaturity, irresponsible behavior, impulsivity, inability to foresee consequences, easily influenced by peers
- Poor self-discipline and lack of study skills
- Very high level of dependency on parents, intense discomfort being away from home, especially overnight
- Your own gut feeling that your child is simply not ready to leave home and meet the challenges of campus life
- Your own gut feeling that you may be setting your child up for failure by sending him or her off to school at this time

For any of the factors delineated above, parents should seriously consider giving their daughter or son the time she or he needs to mature, to stabilize, to be substance-free, to get appropriate medical treatment, and/or to develop the skill set needed to successfully transition to college. Parents should bear in mind that in many countries, a "gap year" between high school and college is very typical, giving young people an opportunity to work, to travel, to volunteer, to become more independent, to take a break from academics, and most importantly, to mature emotionally, psychologically, and academically. In fact, taking a gap year is a trend that is becoming more popular in the United States, as well.[4]

Among the options that parents and students can consider as alternatives to leaving home for full-time college enrollment are the following:

- Living at home and taking one or two courses at a community college. Almost all core courses carry transferable college credits to a four-year college. This allows the student to engage in college-level work at a more manageable pace, and to develop good study habits with less pressure.
- Attending a four-year college while living at home. This allows the more hesitant or less mature student to focus all of his or her energies on academics, without the additional challenges of living away from home. It also allows the young person who is being treated for a psychological or substance abuse problem to continue in treatment with known providers. It further allows for careful medication supervision and monitoring.
- "Stopping out" of school for a year and working full-time with no academic pressure at all. Working full-time will encourage the young person to develop time management skills, stick to a schedule, live within a structure, and generally behave more responsibly.
- The highly dependent young person who has great difficulty separating from home should be strongly encouraged by parents during his or her gap year to venture farther from home, to join activities and groups that take him or her out of the house, to go on overnights, and to travel. In sum, the

gap year should be designed to enhance children's self-confidence in their ability to leave home comfortably and in their capacity to take care of themselves and manage their lives more independently.

In order to comfortably encourage your child to consider not going away to college at age eighteen, you as a parent have to step off the treadmill yourself and let go of the "cosmic timetable." There can be a subtle (or not-so-subtle) competition among parents about where their children are going to school, what successes they are having, and how quickly they are achieving their amazing goals. Although it can be difficult, try not to get caught up in the comparison game. What matters is honestly meeting *your* child where he or she is, and *together* coming up with a plan that will lead to eventual success on a timetable that is appropriate. As a parent, you have the gift of a wider and broader perspective that you can impart to your child.

WHAT IF MY CHILD HAS PSYCHOLOGICAL PROBLEMS?

Parents of children who have previously been diagnosed with a psychological disorder and are receiving effective psychiatric treatment can make their child's transition to college more successful by providing continuity of services for their child. This means making sure that your student's psychiatric care is in place before he or she starts school. Parents reading this before the choice of a college or university has been made may want to make the availability of psychological services on a prospective campus a critical part of your selection criteria.

If no fully staffed on-campus counseling center exists, or if the number of sessions is limited, what are the other options for services outside of the campus? For caregivers reading this after a college has already been selected, this may mean that during the next visit to campus it would be important to seek out and contact the counseling center staff to coordinate the transition of treatment from the at-home provider to one on or near campus. Even if no fully staffed counseling center exists, most schools have a student services department or a treatment coordinator with knowledge about local service providers to whom they refer.

In addition, parents and students can turn to their high school guidance counselor for assistance with the continuity of care. Guidance counselors can contact on-campus psychological services to ascertain the level of care they provide. They can assist the family in researching off-campus mental health care providers, as well as specialized resources for such issues as substance abuse, eating disorders, or self-injury. Your child's high school guidance counselor also has a wealth of information and insight regarding her or his level of functioning in an academic setting.

Even beyond your child's overall level of academic performance, the high school counselor likely has a good handle on his or her level of maturity, self-control, conduct, impulsivity, and general psychological functioning. As with other areas of college selection, parents should not overlook this invaluable source of assistance and honest feedback about your child's readiness for college.

It is recommended that parents be honest about their child's psychiatric history on the campus medical forms. This will provide important information should a crisis arise. Also, children being treated for a psychological disorder should have all previous records transferred to the college counseling center or off-campus provider, once they enter treatment. This will help maintain a good level of continuity of care for them. You should be aware that all treatment information is confidential and is *not* a part of your student's academic record.

In this age of managed care and lack of insurance coverage, parents are advised also to investigate what type of mental health services are covered by either the college insurance or their own existing insurance plan. Some questions to keep in mind include:

- Is there coverage for out-of-state behavioral health services and prescriptions?
- What types of inpatient and outpatient behavioral services are covered?
- Is a referral necessary?
- What types of mental health costs are covered at school by student health fees?

Many students wish to downplay their psychiatric history when starting school. This is very common and understandable. They are experiencing a fresh start, a new beginning at college, and many wish to try out a fresh psychological start as well. This may mean minimizing or denying that a psychiatric history exists. New students may avoid psychological services and not take prescribed medications. However, although the reason for ignoring the psychiatric history is understandable, stopping treatment before or during the transition to school is rarely a good decision.

The transition to college, although positive, can be stressful for many students and can exacerbate underlying psychological disorders, such as depression, anxiety, eating disorders, and problems with alcohol and other drugs. This is why it is especially important to have all psychological and psychiatric resources in place prior to the start of school. Making sure that students have access to some of the critical elements that kept them on track and successful in high school will go a long way toward supporting and maintaining their emotional wellness once they arrive on campus.

In this chapter, we have reviewed some of the significant factors that prospective students and their parents should consider in the process of selecting a college. The importance of the on-campus visit has been highlighted, and sample questions have been posited. Parents have also been asked to consider whether their child is actually ready to start college and especially to live away from home. For parents whose child has already been diagnosed with a psychological disorder, suggestions were offered regarding the continuity of care for a successful transition to college.

In each of these aspects of the college selection process and in assessing their child's readiness for college, parents have been urged to turn to their child's high school counselor and faculty. These high school professionals are superb sources of assistance who can provide guidance, mentoring, insights, and valuable perspectives regarding each of their students.

In the next chapter, many important aspects of the transition to college will be discussed, and recommendations will be offered as to how parents can assist their first-year student in this important process.

Chapter Three

The Transition to College and How Parents Can Help

First-year students undergo changes that are exciting, exhilarating, and challenging. Every aspect of their skills and coping will be tested: their ability to function academically and intellectually at an entirely new level, to create a new social network, to structure their own time, to choose a major, to take responsibility for their lives, to separate emotionally and often physically from home, and to build and solidify their own identity.

For students who are planning to live on campus or on their own, there are the additional demands of caring for themselves in a way that they have never had to do. They may be sharing a room for the first time, adjusting to living with strangers, negotiating differences, indeed even being away for the first time. For students who continue to live at home, there may be a different set of challenges. If there are problems at home, your son or daughter will be affected regardless of where she or he is living.[1]

In this chapter, we will discuss the changes, transitions, and challenges that your son or daughter may encounter during the transition to college, and we will offer suggestions regarding what you can do as a parent to help him or her succeed.

THE IMPORTANCE OF THE FIRST YEAR OF COLLEGE

Long recognizing the significance of a positive experience for first-year students, colleges and universities have devoted considerable resources to promoting academic success, orienting students to their respective institutions, and facilitating their engagement and involvement. The success of the first-year student, academically, interpersonally, and emotionally, bodes well for his or her retention and eventual persistence through graduation.[2] Retention of students through all four years of their undergraduate education is a win-win for all parties concerned—for the institution, for the parents, and, most important, for the student.

Some of the resources that colleges and universities may provide for first-year students include the following:

- Extensive summer orientation experiences that bring students to campus in order to provide activities that facilitate students meeting and connecting with each other, introduce them to faculty and other key persons on campus, inform them about student services, and provide workshops on a variety of issues relevant to student life.
- Intensive first-year experiences, which may include mandatory orientation workshops and advisement meetings; adjustment to college life and academic success courses; and living/learning communities in the residence halls, in which students can have ongoing contact with faculty.
- An abundance of social and cultural experiences that students are invited to at the start of their fall semester.
- Club days and involvement fairs that introduce students to all campus organizations, activities, and volunteer opportunities in a convenient and encapsulated period of time.
- Specifically chosen academic advisers for first-year students, who are particularly adept at connecting with and establishing rapport with them.
- Some campuses have designated deans of the first-year experience with full staffs, who serve as troubleshooters, advocates, and assistants for any roadblock or challenge a first-year student may encounter.
- Many campuses have an office of student retention, which regularly reaches out to first-year students who have been reported by faculty as missing classes and/or struggling academically at midterm.

Here are some suggestions for how you as a parent can assist your first-year student in getting off to the right start:

- It is imperative that your son or daughter attend his or her orientation; if the campus provides an orientation for parents it is very important that you attend as well. You will receive a wealth of information about services available on the campus, nuts-and-bolts information about such areas as financial aid, and an opportunity to meet key professionals on the campus.
- Encourage your first-year student to read the student handbook in order to become familiar with the college code of conduct and with clubs, organizations, resources, student services, and important policies and procedures.

- Encourage your son or daughter to take full advantage of all first-year experience offerings on campus. If the first-year experience is mandatory, encourage your child to take it seriously. If it is optional, encourage your child to participate.
- Many campuses provide workshops on a variety of topics, such as study skills, choosing a major, the transition to college, social skills development, sexual assault, alcohol and other drugs, and stress management. Encourage your son or daughter to take full advantage of these free offerings that can assist him or her academically, personally, and socially.
- Virtually all student services have extensive websites with a wealth of information about such topics as college life, mental health, wellness, safety, and student activities, with links to many more resources. Encourage your first-year student to surf the net regarding his or her own campus resources.

ACADEMIC CHALLENGES

Academically, freshmen inevitably encounter new challenges. Even if your child attended an academically rigorous high school, college will nevertheless be more difficult. For many students, the sheer volume of the work required may well be overwhelming, at least initially. In addition, for the first time, they will be completely responsible for their own learning process; teachers will no longer be reminding them about tests and homework or making sure they are in class every day. From the point of view of the faculty, students are viewed as adults, and they are treated as such. Structuring and managing time is up to them. Getting assignments in on time is entirely their responsibility. For some students, these stepped-up demands are an exciting challenge; for others, it is initially frightening.

As a parent, you should know that although students may spend less time actually in the classroom than they did in high school, they will be required to spend far more time outside of the classroom meeting academic requirements. Although attending every class, taking accurate notes, and being actively engaged are critical for academic success, that is not enough. Students have to develop the self-discipline to set aside substantial blocks of study time and to use them effectively.

We highlight the attribute of self-discipline because it will be indispensable in helping your first-year student navigate and prioritize the many attractive and fun options that will be competing for his or her time and attention. Many colleges and universities front-load exposure to clubs, organizations, and the myriad cocurricular activities available on the campus. They also front-load entertainment, socializing opportunities, and cultural events to engage students through the initial adjustment period and to help them feel at home on the campus. Encouraging students to participate in cocurricular activities is very helpful in connecting students to their campus and engaging them in their college life. In turn, connection and engagement are positively related to student retention and perseverance to graduation.

However, the remarkable number of activities available on the campus immediately challenges students to make discriminating choices about how to apportion their time. Though enriching and enhancing, cocurricular activities will have to be balanced against academic demands. Even more tempting will be the endless opportunities to socialize, hang out, and to just have fun with peers. Further, access to alcohol and other substances will be just an occasional distraction for some students, and it will derail others.

Students who did exceptionally well in high school will automatically assume that they will continue their stellar level of academic performance in college. Many do, in fact, by employing the excellent study habits and self-discipline they applied previously. However, it is not unusual for first-year students to experience a drop in their academic performance during their first semester due to the increased volume of work, as well as issues related to the transition itself. Often after the first semester, they have adjusted and resume their previous level of academic excellence. All students therefore need to have realistic expectations for what their first semester grades will look like. If their performance is well below par, it is recommended that they seek out tutoring and other academic resources on their campus.

An additional challenge for many students will be the financial realities of paying for college, which will require many students to work at paying jobs while in school. Students often feel a profound sense of responsibility to help their families financially, and they are sensitive to not over-burdening their parents. In families in which parents have lost their jobs, students often keenly feel the need to step up by making a substantial financial contribution. Earning money, therefore, becomes a major competing priority that many students must juggle, one that can compromise their academic performance.

In order to meet their academic challenges, students must manage their initial anxiety and panic, manage time effectively, and handle competing priorities, temptations, and responsibilities. Some ways that you as a parent can help your first-year student meet his or her academic challenges are as follows:

- Don't panic when your child does. Know that it is perfectly normal to feel overwhelmed initially by the increased demands. Express confidence in your child's abilities and faith in his or her moving through this initial period of uncertainty.
- Set realistic expectations for your child's academic performance. Pressure from parents creates undue stress and anxiety for students. Be supportive and soothing as your child adjusts to new demands.

- Talk candidly to your son or daughter, even before their coming to college, about the many distractions and temptations on the campus. Let him or her know what you expect, while being realistic about college life. Express confidence in your child's ability to make healthy choices.
- Talk to your student about the difficult topic of academic dishonesty. Certainly your child has heard since first grade that he or she should not "cheat" and is aware that this is unacceptable. In college, however, many students experience intensified competition and pressure to do very well. Therefore, students who have not engaged in this behavior previously may feel tempted to plagiarize or otherwise cut corners in ways that are academically dishonest (and violate campus policy). As a parent you should let your child know that, in addition to being unethical, this behavior carries severe sanctions, including failure in a course, removal from a major, and even expulsion from the institution. Parents need to reassure students that your expectation is that they will simply do the best they can through their own honest efforts.
- Even if your family is going through financial difficulty, reassure your child that his or her priority is being a successful student. Make sure that he or she is not working at an outside job for so many hours that completing schoolwork becomes unfeasible. For your child to be academically successful, he or she needs adequate time to do so.
- If your first-year student remains overwhelmed or anxious, or if he or she has a learning disability or psychological problem that is interfering with academics, strongly encourage him or her to use the student services available on campus. The counseling center, academic resource center, office of student retention, office of the dean of first-year students, and other resources are right on campus precisely to help students to be academically successful.
- If, in spite of your son's or daughter's best efforts and use of resources, he or she continues to struggle academically, there are institutional policies that may offer some relief:

  1. Students should be aware that near the start of a semester they can simply *drop* a class (and add/substitute another if they wish) without penalty.
  2. They should also know that they can *withdraw* from a class well into the semester and earn a grade of "W." Students should check their academic calendar to be clear about what the deadline is to withdraw. Although at that point in the semester a student cannot transfer to another class, if he or she truly believes that earning a passing grade is virtually impossible, withdrawing from the class is strongly advised. It is difficult to overcome a failing grade in terms of maintaining a high overall grade point average (GPA). Parents should be aware that many

students withdraw from a class (or a few classes) over the course of their academic career.
3. Another option open to students who are struggling with a class is to request an "incomplete." Faculty generally grant this request, and schools set a deadline for a completion, usually well into the following semester or trimester. The purpose of allowing students to take a grade of incomplete, is to take the immediate pressure off them and give them a grace period in which they can more comfortably complete their work.

SEPARATION ANXIETY, HOMESICKNESS, AND LONELINESS

Although most students are excited about starting their college careers, the thought of leaving behind the comfort of home, high school friends, and family members can be very stressful. The challenge of making new friends and creating a new social life can be daunting, particularly for the student who is shy. Even if your son or daughter has been looking forward to coming to college and has demonstrated no apprehension prior to his or her arrival, it is not unusual for first-year students to feel somewhat anxious and uncomfortable once they actually arrive on campus. When suddenly confronted with the reality of not seeing family and friends for an extended period of time, some students may become frightened, particularly if they have never really been away from home previously.

Therefore, many students experience some level of separation anxiety and homesickness during the immediate period of transition. For the most part, students who experience homesickness and discomfort about separation will find that these feelings pass after a week or two. They make friends, get involved with activities, and they feel like they are fitting in. But other students may not adjust after a few weeks on campus; instead, they may experience increasing panic and an urgent need to come back home. They may be preoccupied by thoughts about what family members are doing at home and distracted by activities they might be missing. These homesick students may be tearful during their waking hours and have difficulty getting to sleep at night.

An additional challenge for first-year students upon their arrival on campus is that of creating a new social network. For the student who had difficulty making friends and fitting in previously, the transition to college may exacerbate this problem. Even for students who did not have this concern in high school, they may be worried about losing the status they had with peers and daunted by the prospect of starting all over at the bottom of the social ladder, so to speak. Many students will also experience loneliness at this time, the painful feeling that comes from being disconnected from family and friends and not yet having established a new social network. Certainly, students' tolerance for uncomfortable feelings and for spending time alone will be tested upon their arrival on the campus.

Here are some suggestions we have about how you, as a parent, can assist your first-year student in managing the challenges of separation anxiety, homesickness, and loneliness:

- This is the time for parents to do a great deal of patient listening to their son's or daughter's concerns regarding their separation anxiety. It is important to find a balance between panicking, on the one hand, and not taking their distress seriously, on the other. While taking care to let your child know that you genuinely hear how uncomfortable he or she is, it is OK to explain that separation anxiety typically does pass, even though it may feel that it will go on forever.
- Reassure your son or daughter that many people have difficulty with transitions and that the feelings that they are experiencing are perfectly normal and to be expected.
- On a practical level, do encourage your son or daughter to become involved in clubs, organizations, and cocurricular activities, particularly the activities that have been designed for new students. As noted previously, the purpose of these activities is to help students adjust to college, feel more at home, and meet new people.
- Your child may call you urgently requesting to come home. Although it may be painful and difficult to hear your child's distress, encourage him or her to stay at school and not return home immediately. Allowing your child to come home reduces everyone's level of discomfort in the short run; however, it only prolongs his or her separation anxiety.
- Let your child know that his or her resident assistant or other campus helpers are there to offer comfort and support. If your child is convinced that only your actual presence will soothe him or her, and you live close enough to campus, consider a brief visit. Even for the student who is very homesick, simply having parents visit for a few hours or just for dinner can reassure him or her that you are accessible and her or she need not panic.
- In order to build your child's self-confidence during this time of transition, remind your child that he or she has confronted difficult situations in the past and mastered them. Point out that your child has encountered other situations in which he or she had to meet people and make new friends, and has done so successfully. For the student who has had difficulty in this area before, point out that starting college is an opportunity to reinvent himself or herself and that there are resources available to help overcome shyness and develop social skills.

- It can be helpful for all students who are going through a period of loneliness and self-consciousness to know that many of their peers are going through exactly the same situation and dealing with the same challenges. Therefore, your child simply breaking the ice and taking the initiative to start a conversation will probably be received appreciatively by peers.
- Most colleges and universities offer a wide menu of volunteer activities. Many students get involved in these activities to meet other students as well as to serve others. Let your child know that this is an easily accessible way to connect with other students and feel good about making a difference.
- Other simple suggestions include eating in the dining commons rather than in his or her room, and studying in the library or other public places rather than alone. Just being around other students may help pull your son or daughter out of isolation and offer opportunities for conversation.
- Students need to be reminded that during this transition they should remain patient with themselves. It will take time to build friendships; therefore, encourage them not to be dismayed if this doesn't happen immediately. Encourage your first-year student to be persistent and to try a variety of ways to make overtures to others and to connect.
- If over time, your son or daughter continues to feel panicky, lonely, and unhappy, we recommend referring him or her to the counseling center. Many students seek counseling to get support during the transition to college, and typically they can be helped after just a few sessions. If more serious problems emerge that are contributing to making their transition so difficult, the counseling center is exactly the right place for them to be treated for these problems as well.
- If you are unsure as to whether counseling is warranted and/or how to approach your son or daughter about this topic, don't hesitate to call the counseling center for a consultation. A counselor can give you feedback about whether the counseling center is the appropriate student service, and if not, suggest other resources. The counselor can also make suggestions for how to introduce to your child the topic of getting counseling.

IDENTITY DEVELOPMENT

The process of forming a personal identity, one that is individual and separate from the identity of parents, is considered within mainstream American culture to be a normal, healthy developmental process. During late adolescence and emerging adulthood, individuals become more and more their own person, forming and stabilizing their core values, sense of self, spiritual beliefs, political views, and lifestyle choices. At times, emerging adults going through the process of forging their own identities might make choices that parents find puzzling and even worrisome.

In fact, your son and daughter may have already made some personal choices, altered his or her appearance, adopted different values, or developed friendships and relationships in ways that don't necessarily meet with your approval. Nevertheless, many psychologists recommend that, barring truly self-destructive choices, it is advisable for parents to withhold judgment and criticism. For example, the developmental psychologist Erik Erikson suggested that in late adolescence during the stage he called the "identity crisis," parents and other significant adults would do well to declare a "psychological moratorium." He argued that this is precisely the time in life during which it is appropriate for young people to try on different personas, to try out new behaviors, and to push boundaries, in the process of exploring the limits of possible identities.[3]

Sometimes for parents, withholding judgment when their emerging adult becomes a bit unrecognizable to them is very difficult. It might be helpful to know that it is not only necessary for young people to go through this process, it is healthy. As a parent, your being supportive of your child's trying out new experiences and experimenting with new ways to present himself or herself will go a long way toward promoting his or her psychological wellness. For a young person to have parental support and the freedom to solidify his or her identity builds self-esteem, confidence, and self-reliance. Your support, patience, and tolerance during this process, therefore, is an important gift you can give your child.

At the same time, understandably, your son's or daughter's going through this process may require adjustments on the part of all family members, and it may cause a period of disequilibrium. This may be especially true when parents are recent immigrants, first-generation Americans, and/or members of cultures in which strict adherence to traditional values, customs, and religious teachings is expected. As a parent, you should be aware that your son or daughter will be exposed to a contemporary American culture on the college campus that is characterized by lifestyle choices that may be very different from traditional expectations, which you may find to be objectionable. Your son or daughter may, therefore, experience "bicultural stress"—that is, feeling torn between wanting to honor parental/cultural/religious expectations, while also wanting to experience some of the choices that nontraditional peers have access to. It is suggested that, as a parent, you have conversations with your son or daughter about your expectations for cultural or religious adherence prior to their starting college, while appreciating that at times this may be challenging for them.

Regardless of cultural background, an aspect of identity development that some parents may find particularly challenging is that of exploring sexual orientation, and even more challenging may be the exploration of gender identity—that is, one's conception of self as being male or female. During this period of identity development, a relatively small number of individuals may discover that their gender identity differs from their birth sex, and they may eventually identify as transgender. Because one's gender identity and sexuality are such an important aspect of self-definition, it is not surprising that these are issues that individuals would explore during late adolescence and young adult life.

For some college students, this process may be one of affirming a heterosexual orientation and one's birth gender. For others, this process may lead to greater questioning and eventual certainty about a gay, bisexual, or transgender identity. Most colleges and universities offer counseling services, as well as student groups (LGBT student association, gay/straight alliance) that assist students with these aspects of their emerging adult identity. Parents can find information and support through such organizations as Parents, Families and Friends of Lesbians and Gays (PFLAG) and can learn more about their mission and services at http://www.pflag.org. Information about sexual orientation, gender identity, and transgender persons can be accessed on the American Psychological Association (APA) website at http://www.apa.org/topics/sexuality/transgender.aspx.

Here are some additional recommendations that we have for supporting emerging adults as they move through the process of identity development, while also maintaining your own sense of perspective and authority as a parent:

- Know that your son or daughter wants your approval and acceptance during this transitional time. Therefore, be mindful of keeping criticism and negative judgments to a minimum. A lack of acceptance from parents during this time can be damaging to a young person's self-esteem and emerging identity.
- Assume that, during the process of identity development, your son or daughter will make some poor choices and some mistakes. As you know, making mistakes is simply a part of living and growing. Acknowledge to yourself and to your child that you have made mistakes as well and you have survived them. Certainly, help your child to understand that making mistakes is not the end of the world.
- Give your child "wings" during this time—that is, as much freedom as possible (within your cultural framework). Young people should have some latitude with regard to making decisions about friends, values, majors, careers, and personal beliefs in order to become competent adults. Although it is perfectly normal for parents to want to protect their children, overprotection may ultimately be damaging to their development.
- Allow your son or daughter to experience some negative consequences that accrue from making poor choices. Continuously rescuing them robs

young people of the opportunity to understand that every choice they make will have consequences, both good and bad. This is the time of their lives when they need to be able to anticipate consequences and make better choices in light of them.
- Although you may have been in constant contact with your son or daughter via texting, cell phones, and social media, this is probably a good time to contact them less often. Allow them to get through the day without coaching from you, which in turn will help them build their own sense of autonomy.[4]
- Although some of the choices, decisions, and behaviors that your son or daughter engages in during this time of identify development may cause considerable friction in your relationship, be assured that it will likely pass. If you have enjoyed a warm and close relationship prior to your son or daughter entering this period of development, it is likely that you will reconnect and that your bond will endure. On the other hand, if there was friction and discord between you and your child previously, your providing acceptance and affirmation may create an opportunity to become closer and better connected. Certainly, your emerging adult will appreciate your standing by him or her, regardless of the quality of your previous relationship.
- If your son or daughter is, in fact, making self-harmful decisions, such as abusing substances, not attending class, or refusing to respect limits and codes of conduct, do step in and intervene swiftly. A first step would be to contact the counseling center for a consultation about what resources would be most helpful at this time and how to refer your child to them.
- Similarly, if your son or daughter is making choices and engaging in behavior that is unacceptable within your religious or cultural values, talk to your child about this issue as early as possible. Your college or university counseling center will have professional staff sensitive to your culture or religion—who may be members of your cultural or religious cohort—and may therefore be able to serve as consultants or cultural mediators to the family. Alternatively, the counseling center should be able to refer your family to culturally specific and competent sources of assistance.

CHOOSING A MAJOR AND CAREER DECISION MAKING

Many students arrive on the campus with a sense of urgency about choosing a major in order to be on a clear path toward a specific career. Parents, too, may share the expectation that their son or daughter know at the start of college precisely what their professional goals and aspirations are. Certainly there are college students who come to campus with a fairly clear idea of "what they want to do when they grow up." However, for most students, the selection of a major and ultimately of a career is a complex developmental process that takes place over time.

In fact, some would argue that an important objective of a college education is to provide students with exposure to a wide variety of disciplines in order for them to discern where their true interests lie. Further, engagement in cocurricular activities, such as clubs, organizations, on-campus media, and volunteer opportunities allows for further self-exploration with regard to interests, skills, strengths, and priorities.

The interests, priorities, and values of a college student, as an emerging adult, are expected to change and to become more clearly defined, as a function of maturation and of identity development. The career development process, therefore, involves exposure to a wide variety of subject matter, participation in cocurricular activities, and the opportunity to grow in self-awareness and self-knowledge. In addition, college students need considerable knowledge about and exposure to the world of work.

Because of the complexity, as well as the significance, of young persons making good career choices, the one student service that *all* college students should be aware of and make use of is their on-campus career development or planning office—and the sooner the better. Most career development offices offer a wide range of services that can assist college students at every step in their process of choosing a major and ultimately selecting a career. For example, career development offices often offer tests and inventories to assist students in identifying their professional interests, values, priorities, and goals. They also provide access to paid and unpaid internship opportunities and to mentors, as well as assistance with resumé writing, job interviewing, and structuring a job search.

Students' academic advisers, the professors in their courses, and other members of the faculty are other invaluable sources of career information and guidance. Academic advisers inform students about precisely what their course of study will be to meet the requirements for a particular major. Also, at most colleges and universities, faculty members make themselves available to provide information about career options and pathways within their disciplines.

In sum, choosing a meaningful and satisfying career is a complex and often challenging undertaking for the college student. However, career services, academic advisers, and faculty are valuable campus resources that can provide very significant assistance to students throughout this process.

Of course, parents are also of paramount importance as sources of career guidance, support, and information to their college students. Some specific suggestions for how parents can be helpful in this regard are as follows:

- Give your son or daughter the time he or she needs to choose a major and to begin the complex process of career development.

- Offer your advice, personal experiences, wisdom, and guidance—however, without pressuring your son or daughter to pursue the profession that you think is best.
- Bear in mind that selecting a career is one of the most important choices we make in life, and therefore it should be freely chosen and truly meet a complex set of needs, values, and priorities.
- Help your son or daughter with whatever internal sense of urgency, self-imposed pressure, and anxiety that he or she brings to the process. Reassure your college student that it's preferable to take the time he or she needs to make a wise choice.
- Encourage your son or daughter to take full advantage of on-campus resources, particularly the office of career development.
- Encourage your son or daughter to seek out internship experiences, even if they are unpaid; internships can provide on-the-job experience, future job opportunities, and confirmation that this is what your child actually wants to do professionally.
- Encourage your son or daughter to become involved in cocurricular activities that provide useful and relevant professional experience—for example, writing for their college newspaper, doing on-campus radio or television production and broadcasting, being in visible leadership roles, planning complex campus events, or designing and implementing psychoeducational programs for their peers.
- Encourage your son or daughter to explore employment opportunities available on the campus, such as resident assistant, campus minister, student worker, lab assistant, new student orientation leader, or peer educator, which provide valuable professional experiences and exposure.

LIVING ARRANGEMENTS

Regardless of where your son or daughter lives at the start of college—in a residence hall, in an off-campus house or apartment, or at home—he or she will experience unique adjustments and challenges. As a parent, you, too, will encounter new concerns, even if your child lives at home.

For the college student who is leaving home, we have already noted issues of homesickness and separation anxiety. In addition, on-campus residents will have to share a living environment that is often far smaller and more restrictive than what they have been used to. Inevitably, differences among roommates will have to be negotiated, and compromises will have to be made.

Although students have considerable freedom in the residence hall, there are also strict codes of conduct to which they must conform. Violations of the code of conduct carry sanctions, both monetary and disciplinary. The latter can have implications for the student's college career, as egregious violations can result in suspension or expulsion from the residence hall and, in the most serious cases, from the institution.

Students who live off-campus will have to fend for themselves in managing every aspect of their lives, such as shopping for food, cooking, managing a budget, finding transportation, and doing laundry, often for the first time. Further, these students will have no supervision at all, and should roommate conflicts or other problems arise, they will have to be resolved by the student. Because off-campus housing is, by definition, not the property of the college or university, college officials do not have the authority to insert themselves into problems that arise in these settings.

Students who continue to live at home may become more intolerant of curfews, chores, taking care of younger siblings, checking in with parents, and other restrictions and family-related responsibilities that their peers who live away from home are not subjected to. Your formerly compliant and cooperative emerging adult may exhibit resentment and chafe at parental expectations and rules that he or she has not questioned heretofore.

Some recommendations for parents regarding their college student's living arrangements are the following:

- Carefully weigh the wisdom of placing a first-year student in off-campus housing when spaces in on-campus residence halls are available. Even if there is some financial advantage, given the lack of supervision and difficulty for college professionals intervening when problems come up, off-campus alternatives may not be worth the savings.
- Urge your son or daughter to become acquainted with the code of conduct in his or her residential life system and to take sanctions for violations very seriously.
- Encourage your on-campus resident to approach resident assistants and the professional staff of residential life for help with any problem in living that may arise.
- If your college student lives at home, consider easing restrictions and rules regarding such matters as curfews and frequent check-ins, commensurate with his or her entering a new life stage, that of an emerging adult.
- If your college student previously provided significant amounts of child care for younger siblings or other children in your household, lessen your son's or daughter's time commitments; he or she will need to devote much of his or her time to being a successful, involved student.

PROBLEMS AT HOME

For the family that is under duress (for example, as a result of marital problems or a divorce; addiction to alcohol or other substances by a family member; the serious illness of a family member, including grandparents; loss of employment; or other sources of financial strain), it should be assumed that your college student will be affected, regardless of where he or she lives. In fact, sometimes students who are not living at home become even more anxious and distracted, precisely because they don't know exactly what is going on.

With regard to marital conflicts and divorce proceedings, students sometimes feel caught in the middle and compelled to choose sides, a situation that is clearly anxiety provoking and a no-win situation for them. When a family is in financial crisis, students often feel guilty about attending college, viewing it as an indulgence, when they should be working full-time and contributing financially. Similarly, many students experience guilt about not being present for a family member who is ill, as well as anxious about issues related to their treatment and prognosis. Concern for the family member may affect their overall well-being and adjustment to college.[5]

Often students in these challenging family-related situations will not tell their parents about their distress because they don't want to burden family members who are already under duress. Nevertheless, these students do feel the impact, and they may be experiencing such symptoms as anxiety, sleeplessness, depression, and lack of concentration and focus with regard to academics. Students may become so distraught that they stop attending class, completing assignments, or taking tests. Some students may turn to unhealthy coping mechanisms such as self-medicating with alcohol or other substances as a way of ameliorating their distress.

As a parent, you can help your college student better manage and cope with problems at home by:

- Letting your children know that they can always come to you for support, reassurance, and a listening ear.
- Being careful not to put your children in the middle of marital conflicts, and not to engage children as confidants in these matters.
- Reassuring your college student that his or her job is to focus his or her energy on school, even in the face of financial difficulties.
- Assuring your son or daughter that you will keep him or her informed about significant medical issues regarding a sick family member and that you will certainly let your child know if a family member's situation becomes critical. College-aged students should be given the opportunity to say good-bye to terminally ill family members and to be present at the end of a loved one's life, if they choose to do so.

- Encouraging your college student to let professors know that the family is going through a crisis and that he or she may therefore miss class or need an extension on completing an assignment or taking a test. Many faculty members are understanding and compassionate about these situations and will give students a break under these circumstances. Certainly, it is always preferable to let faculty know, rather than to simply miss classes and deadlines without explanation.
- Encouraging your son or daughter to go to the counseling center for support and for assistance with developing coping skills and anxiety reduction strategies to better handle the family crisis.

DIVERSITY AND CULTURAL CHALLENGES

As the population of the United States continues to become increasingly diverse in the twenty-first century, colleges and universities will commensurately reflect our changing, multicultural population. Institutions of higher education view this increase in diversity as an asset that provides exposure to a multitude of cultures, worldviews, and ways of life, which better prepares students to function in an increasingly pluralistic global community. Further, there are several studies that indicate that all students benefit from greater diversity on the campus—academically, interpersonally, emotionally, and vocationally.[6]

On most campuses, "culture" is defined broadly and inclusively, taking in such variables as race, ethnicity, religious beliefs and practices, socioeconomic status, gender, sexual orientation, disabilities and other special needs, nationality, language, age, customs, and rituals. Most campuses recognize the richness and vitality of these differing gifts by creating cultural clubs, organizations, student activities, resources, and extended awareness programs for their college community. Annual commemorations of such national collegiate events as Black History Month, Hispanic Heritage Week, Women's History Month, Coming Out Week, and Lesbian/Gay/Bisexual/Transgender (LBGT) Awareness Week, as well as celebrations of holidays from many religious traditions, have become an integral part of college life on most campuses. In addition, specific majors and courses reflect a growing interest in and focus on the contributions of diverse populations, and in many disciplines, multicultural content is infused across the curriculum.[7]

For those first-year students who come from diverse neighborhoods and/or have attended high schools with a diverse student population, the transition to a multicultural campus and/or living situation should be a smooth and often a welcome occurrence. However, even in our increasingly pluralistic society, many students have not had intensive exposure to cultural diversity in their previous living or learning environment, and for these students, the transition may be challenging.

Some of the situations that students may find particularly challenging include being one of the only visible minority students in a predominantly white classroom; having a roommate who is gay; having a roommate with a physical disability; not finding one's particular culture reflected anywhere on the campus; discovering that not all spaces on campus are physically accessible; hearing other students make racist, sexist, or anti-gay comments; or feeling like a "minority" for the first time in one's life.

Parents can assist their first-year students in meeting diversity-related challenges by:

- Encouraging them to view diversity on the campus as an important and positive part of their learning experience.
- Encouraging participation in a variety of cultural experiences that expand their awareness, sensitivity, and worldview.
- At the same time, encouraging participation in clubs, organizations, and activities within your child's own affinity group, which provides a secure base of support and a sense of belonging.
- If your son or daughter is, or feels that he or she is, different from the majority of students on the campus, encourage him or her to find a mentor to serve as a guide, role model, and resource.
- If your son or daughter feels culturally invisible and unacknowledged on the campus, encourage him or her to advocate for activities, programs, and organizations that recognize his or her cultural identity and needs.
- If your son or daughter has special needs, such as physically accessible spaces, interpreters for the hearing impaired, books on tape, scribes, and so on, encourage him or her to advocate for these accommodations.
- If your son or daughter feels discriminated against, encourage him or her to bring this to the attention of college officials such as the college ombudsperson, and to demand equity.
- Let your students know that they have a right to accommodations and cultural recognition on the campus. Often, when their needs are overlooked, it is due to an omission and lack of awareness on the part of campus professionals, rather than an act of deliberate discrimination. Therefore, once students make others aware of their needs, they will frequently get a positive response.

In sum, colleges and universities want to be responsive to the changing needs and expectations of their increasingly diverse student population. Campus professionals are generally committed to intentionally creating a welcoming and hospitable campus environment in which all students can feel at home and be successful. As a parent, you should know that if your son or daughter is feeling overlooked, discriminated against, or alienated on the campus, there are resources and individuals available for assistance in remedying the situation. A full discussion of these resources and student services may be found in chapter 6.

WHAT IF MY CHILD CONTINUES TO STRUGGLE?

Generally, even those students who are having difficulty with the transition to college do settle down within a few weeks and begin to feel at home and comfortable on their campus. However, some students continue to struggle and may come to realize that the institution they are attending is not right for them for a variety of reasons. Some of the reasons why students would continue to struggle with their transition are as follows:

- They are experiencing homesickness and separation anxiety that does not remit in spite of their efforts to become involved and to speak with a counselor. These students may feel that they are simply not ready to live away from home.
- They entered college convinced that they would pursue a particular major and have changed their minds. The course of study they now wish to pursue is not available on their campus.
- They have a preexisting psychological problem (such as depression, addiction to substances, or an eating disorder) that cannot adequately be managed with campus or community resources.
- They come to believe that the overall culture of the campus is not right for them. Therefore, they have been unable to fit in, connect with peers, or engage in campus activities that appeal to them.
- They discover they cannot manage their life independently without more intense parental supervision and are starting to make poor choices.
- They find that the financial burden and the hours of paid employment needed are impeding their academic performance.

Understandably the situations noted above would be troubling for parents, as all of us anticipate that our child's transition to college will be a positive experience. Here are some ways that parents can assist their child who continues to struggle on the campus:

- Engage your son or daughter in a candid discussion as to what he or she believes is the nature of the problem and how it can best be alleviated.
- Help your student consider such options as commuting from home if possible, dropping a course to relieve pressure, and/or cutting back on paid employment.

- Begin to explore the possibility of your son's or daughter's transferring to another institution that is a better fit.
- Consider the possibility of your child taking a leave of absence for the semester, with the option to return.
- Encourage your student to use campus resources in sorting through these options. For example, a counselor can help the student carefully weigh the consequences of each course of action and suggest additional alternatives.

Parents should be assured that most students who experience difficulty at the start of college eventually find their way. Taking a leave of absence, for example, in no way indicates that the student will not return to school. Parents should also be aware that students may transfer for positive reasons—for example, they find a more cost-effective institution that meets their academic goals, or they do so well academically that they are now eligible for admission to a more prestigious institution.

In this chapter, we have discussed some of the more typical and "normal" challenges students may encounter as they make the transition to college. Some of the expected aspects of this transition include increased academic demands and pressures, homesickness, loneliness and separation anxiety, the process of identity development, a sense of urgency regarding their choice of a major and deciding on a career, and adapting to new living arrangements and an environment that is increasingly diverse and multicultural. In addition, problems related to home and family can arise at any time, and certainly these can have an impact on the academic functioning and psychological well-being of your first-year student. Finally, we addressed the problems of the student who continues to struggle at his or her institution. With regard to each of these issues, we have offered suggestions to assist you in enhancing the emotional, cultural, vocational, and academic wellness of your emerging adult on the college campus.

In the next chapter, parents will be introduced to the realities of current campus life, noting such issues as limited supervision, alcohol and other drug abuse, increasing mental health concerns, sexual assault and harassment, severe roommate conflicts, bullying, bias incidents, and potential violence. It should be noted that most students certainly are *not* subjected to the most traumatic incidents that can occur on the campus. Nevertheless, parents should be aware of them and, equally important, should be prepared to assist and intervene should their child become involved in an untoward incident.

Chapter Four

Today's Campus Environment

What Parents Should Know about the Realities of College Life

To be sure, most students have a wonderful college experience, relishing the opportunity to be in the company of so many interesting and intelligent peers, to pursue their intellectual passions, to have fun, and to have an abundance of stimulating and enjoyable activities to choose from. Never again in life will our students enjoy such a special learning and living environment, dedicated entirely to their growth, development, and entertainment. In the United States today, attending college remains a privilege, and the opportunity to live on or near the campus even more so.

Certainly, there was a time when the campus environment was truly "the ivory tower," a sheltered and protected place that was separate from many of the concerns and problems of "the real world." Students, particularly females, were chaperoned, monitored, and subject to curfews, strict limits in dorm room visitors, dress codes, and rules and boundaries not unlike those that parents would set for their own children.

However, times have certainly changed; there is far less monitoring and considerably more freedom on today's campus. On the positive side, students are asked to be more responsible for themselves and to make good decisions. However, this freedom also creates challenges, and the problems of "the real world" are often very present on the campus. In this chapter, the realities of today's college campus will be explored, including a frank discussion of the kinds of problems your child *may* be exposed to during his or her college years, followed by suggestions for what you can do as a parent to assist your son or daughter to manage these issues, should they arise.

NO IN LOCO PARENTIS

In the not-too-distant past, the college or university considered itself to be *in loco parentis*, that is, functioning "in place of the parent"; however, this is no longer the case. Therefore, the campus, and especially residence halls, no longer have curfews, highly restricted visitation policies, chaperoning, monitoring, single-gender residence halls and floors, and other limits that you might set as a parent. As we have already noted, college students are considered to be adults on the campus, in both the learning and the living environment.

As a parent, you may think that if your son or daughter is living in a residence hall, he or she will be receiving a great deal of monitoring and supervision. However, although residence halls certainly do have clear expectations for living in community and explicit codes of conduct, enforcement is provided for the most part by resident assistants, who are usually undergraduate students themselves. Resident assistants are carefully selected and do have considerable training, but they are essentially the peers of your son or daughter. They will not be making sure that your child attends class, is eating, is cleaning his or her room, or is generally taking care of himself or herself.

You should also know that most residence halls are coed and that many have quite liberal visitation policies. Generally, on-campus residents can visit each other at any time, and many campuses allow residents to have overnight visitors, at least on weekends. Residents do not have curfews, and on many campuses if they are over twenty-one years of age, they can drink alcohol in their rooms, if they wish to do so. On today's campus, residence halls are appropriate for students who can essentially take care of themselves and are inclined to make good decisions and healthy personal lifestyle choices. On-campus residents will experience a considerable degree of freedom, and parents should carefully weigh whether their children are up to handling the responsibility of living without an imposed structure or intensive supervision.

INCREASE IN MENTAL HEALTH CONCERNS ON THE CAMPUS

In absolute numbers, there are more students on the campus with mental health concerns in the last ten years than there were previously. For example, a study by the National College Health Association found that in 2009 a sample of 83,000 students showed that

- 15 percent of all students reported a diagnosis of depression
- of these, 32 percent reported being diagnosed in the past school year

- 25 percent reported current counseling for depression
- 36 percent reported taking medication for depression
- 1.3 percent of all students reported making at least one suicide attempt
- 9 percent of all students reported seriously considering suicide at least once
- 62.1 percent of all students reported feeling hopeless
- 93.6 percent of all students reported feeling overwhelmed
- 91.8 percent of all students reported feeling emotionally exhausted
- 78.8 percent of all students reported feeling so depressed it was difficult to function[1]

This is not to say that there is an increase in mental illness among the general population of eighteen- to twenty-two-year olds. Rather, earlier detection and treatment of mental illness has allowed students for whom entering college might not have been possible previously to now be able to attend. Further, the greater availability of counseling and psychiatric services on the campus has allowed more students to receive some degree of treatment while attending college.

Early detection and greater availability of clinical services are positive developments. However, the severity of the need for intensive, long-term treatment sometimes overwhelms the services available.[2] On many campuses counseling centers have strict session limits, and some do not have psychiatrists on staff to diagnose, to prescribe psychoactive medications, or to monitor their effects. Also, students who have been adequately treated previously, and monitored regarding consistently taking their medication, may choose not to do so at this time. It is not uncommon for students to go off their medications or to stop treatment once they begin college in their desire to "fit in" and to be "just like everyone else." For those students whose academic and social functioning were greatly facilitated by taking psychoactive medication and engaging in treatment, the decision to abruptly stop invariably produces negative consequences.

Therefore, parents should be aware that all campuses today have a population of students with psychological disorders, some of whom are being under-treated or not treated at all. Students who live on campus, even if they are not a part of this population, will likely meet peers who are. Because most college students tend to be caring, compassionate, and helpful, they will often attempt to take care of roommates and other peers with serious emotional problems. While extremely well intentioned, your child can find himself or herself overwhelmed by the problems of others, which may impinge on the quality of your child's life and ability to function optimally as a student.

As a parent, if your own child comes to college with a preexisting psychological disorder, arrange for the continuity of care ahead of time. Be clear about what services are available and to what extent. If you become aware that your child is going beyond compassion and support for a troubled peer, encourage him or her to set boundaries and to redirect the peer to campus services and personnel (such as residential life professional staff and the staff of the counseling center), rather than allowing their own lives to be adversely affected.

ALCOHOL AND OTHER DRUGS

Although residence halls have strict alcohol and other drugs (AOD) policies, and all college events and activities are "dry" for students who are under twenty-one years of age, the availability of substances is nevertheless a reality of campus life. Each year more than eighteen hundred college students die of alcohol- and drug-related overdoses and accidents.[3] Further, the abuse of substances is implicated in such campus incidents as sexual assault, physical assault, hazing, and destruction of property. Abuse of substances also leads to academic consequences such as missing classes, not completing assignments, and even academic failure.

In today's campus culture, binge drinking, intoxication, and their attendant negative behaviors are considered normative and acceptable. The censure by peers of students who are habitually drunk, sick, and inappropriate that was to be expected at one time is no longer the case. In the next chapter, we will discuss the variety of substances that your son or daughter may be exposed to. For the purposes of this discussion, however, we want to heighten parents' awareness that this is a serious problem that campuses are continually struggling to address, albeit with varying degrees of success. As a parent, you are encouraged to frankly discuss issues related to alcohol and other drugs with your child and to recognize signs that your student may be abusing substances, which will be clearly delineated in the next chapter.

SEXUAL ASSAULT

Although, in general, college students are less likely to become victims of violent crime than their eighteen- to twenty-two-year-old counterparts who are not in school, the one exception is sexual assault, particularly acquaintance rape. In fact, parents should be aware that female college students are the most likely cohort in the United States to be victims of rape.[4]

Often, young women come to the campus assuming that residence halls are absolutely safe, that peers and classmates are always to be trusted, and that bars and restaurants in the immediate vicinity of their campus are safer than other such establishments. Unfortunately, this is not necessarily the case. As noted above, the availability of alcohol and other drugs is strongly implicated in instances of rape on the campus. Studies on rape and college students show that in over 80 percent of cases, one or both parties are intoxicated. Further, coed residence halls and liberal visitation policies inadvertently allow extraordinary access to potential victims, as well as a false sense of security on the part of entering students. In addition, the presence of trusting, vulnerable young people on or near the college campus makes these environments a hunting ground for predators.

Many colleges provide programs to educate students about the realities of rape on or near the campus. These educational programs alert students to the problem, make specific suggestions for them to be less vulnerable (such as locking their doors, not accepting drinks from strangers, not becoming intoxicated, not going off with people they don't know, and not leaving a friend behind in a compromising or unsafe situation). These programs also tell students what to do and where they can receive help in the event that they or a friend has been raped. In addition, many campuses have rape crisis hotlines and counselors available for students.

Most colleges and universities have voluntarily promulgated policies explicitly prohibiting sexual violence on the campus and provide prevention workshops, websites, and other resources. Parents should be aware that in April 2011, the Campus Prevention Elimination Act or Campus SaVE Act, (S.834), was introduced in the U.S. Senate, which will underscore the responsibility of colleges and universities to provide primary prevention with regard to all forms of campus sexual violence, including sexual assault, domestic violence, dating violence, and stalking. New federal guidelines were also issued in April 2011 with regard to holding institutions to a higher standard when investigating sexual assault incidents on the campus. Parents can learn more about these guidelines issued by the U.S. Department of Education Office of Civil Rights by accessing its "Dear Colleague Letter: Sexual Violence" at http://www.whitehouse.gov/sites/default/files/fact_sheet_sexual_violence.pdf.

It is hoped that more intense scrutiny and oversight by the federal government will yield a reduction in the incidence of sexual assault (and other forms of interpersonal violence) on the campus. However, currently, it is reported that 20–25 percent of college students are victimized. Sadly, students are sometimes assaulted as soon as they arrive on campus or shortly thereafter. They may not yet have been educated about this danger and/or they are simply distracted by the demands of adjusting to college.

We encourage parents to talk to their children frankly about this issue prior to their arrival on the campus. In addition to safety tips for potential victims, all students should know that clear consent is needed for all physical activity and that not receiving consent because the other person is too intoxicated to give it meets the legal definition of rape. Many health services, counseling centers, or campus safety and security websites provide explicit information for students regarding this topic.

As a parent, this is some specific information that it would be useful for you to know. Date rape occurs when sex is forced on someone by a person they know socially—for example, a friend, boyfriend, or a new acquaintance. The perpetrator is usually male and may use physical and verbal threats, emotional blackmail, or alcohol and drugs to force or manipulate the other person into having sex. The abuse may include sexual intercourse, oral sex, or inappropriate or unwanted touching. Date rape can happen to both men and women, but just as with other forms of sexual assault, young females between the ages of sixteen and twenty-four are at highest risk. On the college campus, it is reported that 90 percent of sexual assaults are perpetrated by assailants known to the victim.[5]

The emotional consequences of date rape may be very serious and enduring. As with other types of rape, the victims often report feeling frightened, traumatized, and distrustful of others. They may become hesitant to form new relationships and may have lifelong fears about intimacy. Some victims become so distraught about encountering their assailant that they leave school. For many victims there is the risk of developing posttraumatic stress disorder, particularly if they do not receive psychological help and treatment.

If your child is male, he should nevertheless be concerned and educated about acquaintance rape and sexual assault. Because males are often perpetrators, it is important to let your son know that without clear consent, he can be accused of acquaintance rape and held accountable even if he and his partner are intoxicated. In addition, males can be victims themselves, and therefore, they too should be cautioned to keep themselves safe and to have their wits about them in social situations, particularly when alcohol is involved.

If your child is a female, as a parent, please let her know that she is particularly at risk for acquaintance rape at the start of school. Encourage her to socialize in groups and discourage her from going off with someone she doesn't know. Remind your daughter that she does not "owe" sex to anyone on a date in exchange for dinner or other courtesies. Let your daughter know that people who use coercion, manipulation, and force are not potential romantic partners, and they certainly do not have her best interest at heart.

Discussing date rape with your child may not only serve to prevent an assault but can also make it easier for him or her to talk to you should an assault occur. If your child is a victim of a sexual assault:

- Tell him or her to get help immediately. Instruct your child to go to a hospital, a rape crisis center, or a physician's office.
- Remind your son or daughter not to blame himself or herself. Take care not to make blameful statements yourself, such as "Why did you go off

alone with a boy in the first place?" or "What do you mean you were too drunk to fight back?" Students are sometimes reluctant to confide in their parents about rape because they are fearful of being blamed for the assault.
- Let your child know that you can handle bad news and that it's your role to help him or her through difficult events. At times, students will not disclose traumatic incidents to their parents for fear of hurting them and out of a desire to protect them.
- Don't force your child to talk about the details with you. For some victims of rape, having to relive the event is retraumatizing. Also, many students are embarrassed, and they often have a wish to protect their parents from hearing the disturbing details.
- In a nonthreatening, supportive way, let your child know she or he can consider pressing charges. Campus authorities and the police should be notified even if the student does not wish to press charges. Rapists usually rape again; your child's information can help past or future victims of the same perpetrator who do wish to press charges. Let your child know that victims who report incidents of rape tend to recover much more fully than those who do not report or attempt to impose consequences for this crime.
- Encourage your student to get counseling to talk out his or her feelings now and to prevent long-term psychological problems in the future. Victims who engage in counseling tend to heal much more fully than those who do not.

DATE RAPE DRUGS

Date rape drugs are powerful and dangerous substances sometimes used to perpetrate a sexual assault. Typically, the drugs used include Rohypnol, or "roofies," and similar substances such as gamma hydroxybutyrate (GHB), which leave individuals extremely vulnerable to sexual assault. They can be used on both male and female victims.

Date rape drugs are sometimes put into drinks without the person's knowledge. These drugs have no taste, odor, or color, so they are difficult to detect. These drugs make victims weak or confused, so that they are unable to refuse sex or defend themselves. Once the person is drugged, he or she usually does not remember what happened during that time.

Date rape drugs usually begin working about ten to twenty minutes after ingestion. The victim may begin to feel disoriented, dizzy, and occasionally nauseous. The person may have difficulty speaking and/or moving and may pass out. The drug's effects can last anywhere from two to eight hours, and there is usually no recollection of what occurred. These drugs can also pose serious health risks, which include liver failure, seizures, potentially fatal respiratory problems, and coma. Occasionally, rather than becoming sedated and passing out, individuals may become extremely agitated, belligerent, and aggressive.

The following suggestions are offered for how parents can educate their children:

- Make sure they are aware of date rape and date rape drugs.
- Let them know that they should not drink anything they did not open themselves or did not see being opened.
- Caution them to never accept a drink from someone they don't know well.
- Urge them to always watch their drink at parties and bars and never leave their drink unattended.
- Encourage them to have a friend or group of friends with whom to go to and from parties or bars.
- Suggest that they never leave friends who seem disproportionally intoxicated alone; they may have been given a date rape drug.
- Let them know that as the evening progresses they should keep alert for which of their friends are still present, so they can have a safe companion for the trip home.
- Urge them to never accept a ride from or go home with someone they don't know well.

Although date rape drugs tend to cause amnesia about the events that occurred while the individual was under their influence, there may be evidence of sexual assault on the person of the victim and/or in the environment. Also, friends may raise concerns with the victim about what may have taken place. Students should know that if they feel strange, disoriented, or disproportionately drunk after ingesting alcoholic beverages, they should consider the possibility that a drug may have been slipped into their drink. If they suspect that they may have been slipped a date rape drug, students should know to do the following:

- Take their suspicions very seriously and act on them.
- If possible, try to keep a sample of the drink for analysis.
- If sexually assaulted, they should not shower or otherwise destroy evidence. They should go to a hospital immediately to have a medical examination and collection of evidence. This does not mean they will necessarily have to press charges against the assailant. However, should they decide to press charges, the evidence will have been preserved.
- Students who are unsure regarding whether they have been sexually assaulted should nevertheless go to an emergency room to be tested for the presence of a date rape drug and/or for evidence of sexual assault or an STD.

- Recommend and encourage students to get support to help them through the traumatic event. Encourage them to reach out to people they trust for support and to get professional assistance from the counseling center or an off-campus agency.

UNHEALTHY RELATIONSHIPS

The opportunity to meet new people and to develop a friendship or romantic relationship is one of the most exciting parts of going to college. This aspect of college life should be fun and enhancing to a student's self-esteem. Unfortunately, sometimes students find themselves in relationships that provide the converse. Instead of being healthy and enjoyable, the relationship makes them unhappy and anxious. These relationships may involve fighting, conflict, and even violent behavior. Studies of dating relationships on the college campus reveal that at least 30 percent of college students have experienced emotional or physical relationship abuse themselves, and 70 percent know someone who has been in an abusive relationship.[6]

As a caregiver, it is normal to wonder about the types of relationships your child will be involved in. Now that your child is at school, he or she will have more freedom to develop and to manage relationships on his or her own. As a result, you will likely have less opportunity to see firsthand the people with whom your child is socializing and getting close to than you did previously.

As a parent it is important to make sure that your child understands the basic principles of healthy and unhealthy relationships so that, regardless of what his or her experience has been at home, he or she has a point of reference for evaluating new relationships. The first step in determining how to create a healthy relationship is understanding what constitutes healthy ways of relating. Below are some key concepts:

- There is little emotional pain in the relationship.
- There is mutual respect. Partners are treated as equals in the relationship.
- Partners respect each other's right to privacy and respect boundaries. In today's culture, that means not reviewing each other's phone records, e-mails, texts, and other private information without permission.
- Partners trust each other and consider the other to be their best friend.
- Partners are genuinely interested in each other's feelings, opinions, and interests.
- Partners make an effort to meet and to include each other's family and friends.
- The relationship provides emotional support, especially during difficult times.

- Partners do not manipulate or control each other.
- The physical relationship is one in which both partners feel comfortable; there is never any use of manipulation, coercion, or pressure to be sexual.
- Arguments or disagreements are resolved respectfully. There is more interest in finding a resolution than in one person "winning." In fact, open conflict is relatively rare in the relationship.
- Partners support and encourage each other to be successful and achieve their goals.
- Negative emotions are handled without verbal or physical abuse.
- Neither partner abuses substances.
- Neither partner has difficulty managing anger or respecting boundaries.

An abusive relationship can be defined as a pattern of physical or psychological control that one person exerts over the other in order to get his or her own way. The behavior physically or emotionally harms the other person, creates anxiety and fear, demeans the person, prevents the person from doing what he or she wants, or makes them behave in ways they have not freely chosen. Warning signs of an unhealthy and abusive relationship include the following characteristics:

- Anger, fighting, name calling, and "drama" are frequent occurrences.
- Mental, verbal, and/or physical abuse are present in the relationship.
- Partners are isolated and have no support system outside of the relationship.
- Partners feel controlled and monitored; they have lost their sense of privacy.
- Partners are chronically disappointed and frustrated in the relationship.
- There is obsessive texting and intense and anxious excessive contact.
- There is no trust and constant jealousy.
- There is fear and a sense of walking on eggshells.
- Partners are restricted in relating to others and have to constantly account for their time and whereabouts.[7]

If you suspect that your child is in an unhealthy relationship, tell him or her directly that you feel this way. Whenever possible, give specific examples of why you believe this to be true. Let your child know that he or she should not tolerate bad behavior, that love shouldn't hurt, and, that your child deserves better. Take care not to attack the character of the abusive partner but to discuss the behavior that causes a problem for your child. In addition, let your child know that you will support his or her decision to end the relationship. Recommend that your child contact the counseling center to explore why he or she is in this relationship, as well as ways to extricate himself or herself from an abusive situation.

SEXUAL HARASSMENT ON CAMPUS

Sexual harassment of students by peers, faculty, or staff is another problem that sometimes arises on the college campus. Most frequently females are victimized; however, men can be victims of sexual harassment as well. Sexual harassment describes a continuum of behaviors that varies from repeated sexually embarrassing remarks or innuendos to physical assault. It may involve explicit or implied threats to the student's academic success, job performance, or safety. Sexual harassment can make a student's academic or living environment increasingly uncomfortable through continued sexual comments, suggestions, or pressures.

Sexual harassment may include unwanted behaviors such as

- pressuring someone to go out for drinks, dinners, dates
- invading personal space while working and socializing
- telling off-color jokes
- making obvious and inappropriate sexual gestures
- asking inappropriate questions about an individual's personal and/or sexual life
- displaying sexually suggestive photos, graffiti, or other materials
- putting pressure on or coercing a person into sexual interaction
- attempting to kiss or touch without consent
- pressuring someone to disclose their sexual orientation

Persons victimized by sexual harassment often are pressured by persons who exert some control or power over them in a social relationship, in an academic program, or in the workplace. Sexual harassment can be in the nature of quid pro quo—for example, the promise of a better grade in exchange for sex. However, most often it takes the form of creating a hostile environment, which creates sufficient discomfort to interfere with the student's ability to function adequately in his or her living, learning, or work environment.[8]

Parents are encouraged to talk to students about sexual harassment. As described above, let them know clearly what it is, and that it is something that can happen on campus or at work. Let them know that it is not their fault, that they should not tolerate it, and offer guidance about what they can do if it occurs. Sometimes sexual harassment can be stopped by having the student take direct action. Students can tell their harasser they find his or her behavior inappropriate and ask that it cease immediately. In most cases, avoiding or ignoring the harassment will not make it go away. Instruct the student to keep a written record of what has happened. The record should include a detailed description of what took place (who did and said what to whom), the time, the place, and the names of people involved and of witnesses. This record can serve as a powerful resource should your son or daughter wish to file a formal complaint.

It is understandable that a student may be reluctant to talk about his or her experience. This reluctance is normal and may have several causes:

- uncertainty about what is harassment and whether or not he or she has really been harassed
- feelings of shock or embarrassment over the incident
- believing that he or she caused or deserved the harassment
- fear that the complaint won't be taken seriously
- fear of retaliation

Most colleges and universities have an ombudsperson who has been specifically trained to deal with complaints of sexual harassment. Many students prefer to involve the ombudsperson rather than deal with a harasser on their own. The ombudsperson usually will review what has happened from the student's perspective and discuss the options available so that the student can make an informed decision about the best course of action. The ombudsperson will let your child know all of his or her options, both on and off campus, including informal, formal, and legal venues for filing a grievance or a complaint. In addition, the ombudsperson will make every effort to protect your son's or daughter's privacy and to protect him or her from retaliation.

ROOMMATE CONFLICTS

Although there are adjustments and often compromises inherent in living with a roommate, for the most part this process should be smooth and relatively painless. Students should be able to negotiate differences regarding such issues as bedtime, quiet time for studying, borrowing clothes, using each other's property, privacy, and inviting visitors to their room.

However, at times, roommates have difficulty negotiating differences, and prolonged conflict may ensue. For example, roommates may have serious values conflicts about such issues as alcohol and other drug use, sexual behavior (especially if it takes place in a shared room), hygiene and cleanliness, or their respective levels of tolerance for continuous personal crises and drama. Also, a situation may arise in which your son or daughter may feel excluded from social activities, dinner invitations, and other interactions among other roommates or suitemates. At times, students in this situation feel deliberately shunned or isolated.

If your son or daughter cannot reach a resolution with, or find a way to be included by, his or her roommates, encourage the involvement of a resident assistant in mediating the situation, a strategy that is often effective. In more serious conflicts, encourage your child to approach a member of the residential life professional staff such as a hall director or area coordinator for assistance. The professional staff in residential life typically has a great deal of experience and expertise in helping roommates resolve conflicts. Off-campus residents can contact the counseling center for consultation about how to manage conflict with roommates.

Some suggestions for how parents can assist with roommate conflicts are as follows:

- Parents should encourage their children to use campus resources, rather than the parents' getting directly involved in all but the most serious situations.
- Even in conflicts of a more serious nature, parents are admonished against directly confronting their child's roommate or suitemate in person, via e-mail, text messaging, on Facebook, or by any other means. It is inappropriate for parents to get into their own conflict with adolescent students who are not their children. Instead, parents should consult with residential life professional staff or other campus professionals about how to best resolve the situation.
- As a parent, you should know that if your son or daughter cannot resolve the conflict and/or finds the living situation intolerable, he or she does have the right to request a room change. Please bear in mind that the request for a room change must come directly from the student himself or herself.

PRIVACY IN CYBERSPACE

As a parent of an adolescent, you are already aware of the danger of conducting much of one's life in cyberspace. No doubt your child is on Facebook and other social websites, on which she or he posts a great deal of information as well as many photos. Your child already texts continually (even when the recipient is close by) and often sends picture texts.

While your son or daughter lives under your roof, you are able to provide at least *some* oversight over their activities in cyberspace. No doubt you have already warned your child about the do's and don'ts of what to post online, and you certainly have warned him or her about meeting people off-line whom they have met only in cyberspace. You also likely know that many teens who are otherwise responsible disregard their parents' warnings and make poor decisions regarding their behavior in cyberspace.

A growing concern with regard to teens and young adults is the practice of sexting. This is a prime example of otherwise responsible young people making very poor choices with regard to safeguarding their privacy. Sexting involves sending or forwarding nude or sexually suggestive photos, as well as sexually explicit comments online or on a cell phone.

As a parent, you may be surprised to learn that a recent study found that 20 percent of teens (age 13–19) and 33 percent of young adults (age 20–26) have sent, or posted online, nude and/or seminude photos or videos of themselves. In addition, in this study 39 percent of teens and 59 percent of young adults reported sending or posting sexual messages.[9] Another study confirmed that, among college students, more than half of those surveyed reported that they have received sexual images, and almost 80 percent reported receiving sexually suggestive text messages. In addition, a significant percentage of young adults reported seeing sexual images and messages not intended for them and/or forwarding sexual images and messages to unintended recipients.[10] Also, young people, especially females, reported feeling pressured to engage in sexting and reported being more sexual than they would be in real-life situations.[11]

For young people who share images of teens who are under eighteen years of age, there are growing legal implications and consequences, including being accused of and prosecuted for sending child pornography, and ultimately being required to register as a sexual offender, in some cases.

Although you likely have already spoken to your children about the dangers in cyberspace, their departure to college would be a good time to review cyberspace safety guidelines with them.

Some recommended safety guidelines are as follows:

- Keep your password private. There is no reason for any peer, including a romantic partner, to have that information.
- Protect identifying information about yourself, including your address, your school, and your whereabouts. Use privacy settings—they are there for a reason.
- Don't post any images or comments about yourself that you would not share in real life.
- Don't post comments about others that you would not comfortably say to their face.
- Be aware that sexual images and comments that you send or post can be forwarded to unintended recipients (and they often are). These images exist in cyberspace forever. Do you really want them out there?
- Similarly, don't forward private or sexual material sent to you.
- Don't allow yourself to be pressured by peers, including romantic partners, to post or send sexual images of yourself.
- Visit such websites as http://www.athinline.org to learn more about safety in cyberspace.[12]

In this section we have discussed ways that students can cause harm to themselves in cyberspace by disregarding their own privacy and personal boundaries. In the next section, we will discuss ways that students sometimes cause harm to others by violating the boundaries and privacy of others.

BULLYING AND CYBERBULLYING

The topics of bullying and cyberbullying have long been on the agenda and in the awareness of the general public with regard to middle school and high school students. More recently, a number of high-profile incidents that resulted in negative consequences for college students, including loss of life, have made campus professionals aware that these topics are very relevant for a college student population, as well.[13]

It is important for parents to distinguish between roommate conflicts and bullying, which is far more serious in nature. Roommate conflicts tend to arise from genuine differences in lifestyle habits, values, preferences, and choices of friends that may cause friction between individuals occupying the same relatively small space. Bullying, on the other hand, involves the *deliberate* infliction of psychological or physical harm aimed at an identified target. Bullying can involve deliberately and repeatedly making negative and demeaning comments; intentionally shunning, avoiding, and excluding an individual; deliberately destroying property; and, ultimately, the infliction of physical harm.[14]

On the college campus, one of the most common forms of bullying is cyberbullying or cyberharassment, which involves the use of information and communication technologies for the purpose of deliberate, repeated, and hostile behavior with the intention of harming another person. Examples include demeaning, humiliating, threatening, intimidating, or manipulating an intended victim. Methods of cyberbullying or harassment include the use of Facebook, Twitter, Skype, e-mail, message boards, gossip sites, cell phones, text messages, and other social networks.[15]

A particularly egregious use of technology for the purpose of humiliating or embarrassing a college student involves the violation of privacy. For example, victims may be surreptitiously videotaped or audiotaped during private or intimate moments and then discover that these have been shared or broadcast widely. In addition, private and personal information, photos, and other materials can be exposed in ways that are not only humiliating, but also damaging, to the victim.

Another misuse of the Internet that is harmful to students involves cyberstalking for the purpose of meeting a person that one intends to victimize, embarrassing a person, or obsessively monitoring them. For college students, electronic media can be used to control, threaten, or intimidate a partner in an unhealthy relationship. For example, a student can use constant text messaging to control a partner's whereabouts. He or she can invade the privacy of a partner by monitoring their use of cell phones, e-mail, and social networking sites. The Internet can also be used to intimidate or coerce a partner, or to threaten exposure of embarrassing information. In the case of a breakup, electronic means can be used to make it frightening or feel unsafe for an individual to leave a relationship.

Cyberbullying, harassment, and stalking are particularly alarming in that often the perpetrator cannot be positively identified and therefore feels safe in harming peers without fear of consequence. However, there are certainly consequences for the victim, including fear, anxiety, depression, and humiliation.

As a parent, you should know that many campuses are becoming aware that this is a problem and are implementing programs that educate students on the topic of cyberbullying, cyberstalking, and cyberharassment. College campuses are attempting to empower victims to report these incidents and to insist on consequences. College codes of conduct are starting to specifically address this topic and to impose sanctions.

A promising strategy that an increasing number of colleges and universities are implementing is bystander intervention training. These are evidence-based training programs that empower students to intervene in instances of bullying and cyberbullying (as well as other situations that are interpersonally damaging such as acquaintance rape, hate speech, physical violence, or domestic violence) in order to prevent or interrupt these behaviors. Parents can learn more about bystander training at http://www.stepupprogram.org or at http://www.livethegreendot.com.

The following suggestions are offered for parents whose child finds himself or herself in the unfortunate predicament of being bullied, cyberbullied, harassed, or stalked:

- Let your son or daughter know that all of these activities constitute very serious infringements of the student code of conduct and should be reported, for example, to a resident assistant, a member of the residential life professional staff, campus safety and security, or a dean.
- Let your son or daughter know that he or she has a right to expect an investigation of these incidents and, if confirmed, to anticipate the imposition of clear sanctions and consequences against the perpetrators.
- Tell your son or daughter to save e-mails, text messages, and other evidence that would substantiate their claim.
- If your son or daughter has exhausted all appropriate channels and the bullying continues, this is an instance in which it is appropriate for parents to become involved and to directly request action from campus professionals.

- Encourage your son or daughter to go to the counseling center in order to seek out support and advocacy in these situations.
- Encourage your student to become involved in bystander intervention training initiatives on his or her campus.

HAZING

Hazing may be viewed as a form of institutional bullying. It is defined as "any activity expected of someone joining or participating in a group that humiliates, degrades, abuses, or endangers them regardless of a person's willingness to participate."[16] Although campus policies and some state laws and regulations explicitly prohibit hazing, it continues to take place on some college campuses. Students may experience hazing in connection with pledging a fraternity/sorority and/or becoming a member of an athletic team, a club, or another student organization.

Examples of hazing include verbal and physical abuse, threats, demeaning assignments, name calling, meaningless repetitive activities, sleep deprivation, social isolation, humiliation, and inducements to drink at dangerous levels or to participate in other high-risk activities. As a parent you should know that 55 percent of college students involved in the types of organizations noted above experience hazing, but they almost never report it. Often victims believe that these hazing experiences are a necessary part of the initiation and bonding process with their organization.[17]

Although some students are compliant with regard to hazing, they nevertheless can experience negative consequences. For example, they may experience a retraumatization of a past event, stress, anxiety, paranoia, depression, loss of control, and difficulty with concentration. Some students may experience these symptoms without fully recognizing that they have been the victims of hazing.

Parents should be aware that most colleges and universities provide anti-hazing workshops and make attendance mandatory for some student cohorts. Parents can also educate their student about the possibility of being hazed and its consequences. Parents should let their son or daughter know that these behaviors are harmful, a violation of campus policy, and usually illegal. If a parent believes that their student is displaying troubling symptoms of hazing, they should refer him or her to counseling. The student should also be informed that these behaviors can be reported to college officials, to the NCAA, and/or to the national fraternity or sorority organization.

BIAS INCIDENTS

A particularly ugly and insidious form of bullying, harassment, and intimidation on the college campus involves the deliberate perpetration of a bias incident or even a hate crime. These incidents may target a specific student, a group of students, or members of a particular religion, race, ethnicity, nationality, sexual orientation, or other minority or nonprivileged cohort. Although the number of bias crimes has significantly decreased on the campus over the past several decades, as a parent you should know that they do continue to take place. Examples include writing racial or ethnic slurs in public spaces, on message boards, or on other property of individual students. It also involves the use of hate symbols such as nooses or swastikas, and making death threats against individuals or groups of individuals based on their minority status. Bias incidents and hate crimes can also take the form of hate speech, in which clearly racist, sexist, homophobic, anti-Semitic, or otherwise offensive comments are made directly to or about individual students or groups of students.

All campuses have codes of conduct that prohibit these behaviors and impose sanctions and consequences on perpetrators. If your son or daughter has been targeted, this is an instance in which you, as a parent, should become involved. Understandably, targeted students become fearful for their safety and feel shunned and, at times, isolated within their campus community. Sometimes it is helpful for them to spend some time at home in the aftermath of these incidents in order to be in a safe space and to regain their equilibrium. Upon their return to school, it is recommended that targeted students seek counseling for support, advocacy, and healing. Parents should also empower their son or daughter to demand action, including a thorough investigation, apprehension of perpetrators, and imposition of consequences for their behavior.

CAMPUS VIOLENCE

Although incidents such as campus shootings involving multiple victims have received a great deal of media attention in recent years, in fact college campuses are relatively safe with regard to violent crimes. College students are less likely to be victimized in a violent crime than their non-college student counterparts, with the exception of acquaintance rape.

Furthermore, since high-profile campus tragedies have been perpetrated, many colleges and universities have taken steps to better safeguard their communities. For example, many campuses provide information and training to all constituencies, including students, faculty, staff, and administrators, on recognizing signs and symptoms of potentially dangerous individuals. In addition, many campuses have set up interdisciplinary groups of professionals, such as students of concern committees or threat assessment teams, in order to be a clearinghouse for information about potentially disturbed or violent students. Any member of the campus community can inform these groups about individuals of concern, and the community member can remain anonymous, for the most part, as a reporter. Students of concern committees and threat assessment teams will weigh the known risk factors about a given individual and determine a course of action, which might include a mandatory evaluation, a referral for psychological treatment, disciplinary sanctions, suspension or expulsion from the campus, or the involvement of law enforcement.[18]

Many campuses have also set up alert mechanisms to inform all members of the community about possible or actual threatening situations taking place on campus. Colleges often use a text-messaging system, which necessitates that all members of the campus community register their cell phones with a designated office or on a designated website. All registered persons will then receive a text message informing them of a dangerous or threatening situation, with instructions intended to promote their safety.

With regard to other crimes that target students, the campus police or office of campus safety and security often provides programs, websites, and written materials informing students on how to keep themselves and their property as safe as possible. You should also know that, by law, under the Cleary Act, all colleges and universities must report all crimes that have taken place on or near their campus on an annual basis. This information is a matter of public record, and therefore parents and students can access information regarding the number and nature of crimes that have taken place on their respective campuses.

As a parent, here are some suggestions for assisting your children to be as safe as possible on the campus:

- Urge them to access and read materials provided by their campus safety experts. This information typically runs the gamut from commonsense suggestions like keeping the door locked whenever they are out of the room to how to respond in case of a fire, the presence of a violent individual, or other significant threats to the campus.
- Make sure that they are using the campus alert mechanism, for example, by urging them to register their cell phone for the purpose of emergency notification.
- Let them know that there is likely a clearinghouse on their campus, such as the students of concern committee or threat assessment team, that is designated to receive information from campus constituents about members of the community that they believe pose a threat to self or others.

- With regard to an individual who may pose a threat to the campus, some of the warning signs that students should be aware of include making direct threats of violence; displaying an inability to manage anger; a history of violence; inappropriate behavior in the classroom or in the residence halls; and/or using e-mail, text messages, Facebook, or away messages to hint at violence.

In the next chapter we will more fully discuss the signs and symptoms of the potentially dangerous student, as part of a larger discussion of psychological problems encountered on the college campus. In this chapter, we have alerted parents to the kinds of problematic situations their son or daughter might encounter on the campus, ranging from roommate conflicts to the far more serious problems of bias incidents or violence.

Clearly, many, if not most, students will *not* encounter these situations. Parents can foster their children's emotional and physical wellness by talking to them about these issues in an effort to prevent their children becoming victimized or embroiled in untoward relationships and situations. Parents can also foster wellness by being supportive and non-blaming, and by knowing when to step in, if their child is victimized on the campus. Finally, parents should not hesitate to direct their children to on-campus resources, and to consult those resources as needed, if a difficult situation does arise. On-campus resources and student services will be discussed in chapter 6.

In the next chapter, parents will learn about some of the psychological disorders, as well as problems with alcohol and other drugs, that college students sometimes experience.

Chapter Five

Recognizing Signs of Psychological Problems, Chemical Dependency, and Addictive Behavior

What Parents Need to Know

Because there has been an increase in unhealthy behaviors and psychological disturbance on the college campus, and because parents remain the primary resource that their children turn to, it is beneficial for parents to understand the nature and symptoms of psychological disorders and addictive behaviors that can develop during the college years. Parents who have this basic understanding will be better able to recognize whether their child has a problem in order to access help that is appropriate and effective.[1]

In this chapter, parents will be provided with an overview of the psychological problems that can arise during the college years. Some of the more common problems that will be reviewed include depression, anxiety disorders, eating disorders, and responses to loss or trauma. We will also present less common problems that nevertheless may arise in college-age students, including bipolar disorder, suicidality, schizophrenia, violent behavior, problems with anger and aggression, and self-injurious behavior. In addition, substances that students may abuse will be discussed, and symptoms of addictive behavior will be presented. Finally, recommendations for parents will be delineated with regard to talking to their children about psychological problems and addictive behaviors.

DISORDERS OBSERVED IN COLLEGE-AGE STUDENTS

Depression

It is the hope of parents and campus professionals that all students will have a positive and productive experience during college. Yet statistics show that among eighteen- to twenty-four-year olds, depression is a fairly common occurrence. This means that there is a good chance a college student may encounter this difficulty, in either himself or herself or with a friend or roommate. Coping with depression can be difficult for both the person experiencing the mood disturbance and for the friends and family of the individual. It can be especially challenging when thoughts of self-harm accompany a depressive episode.

Depression involves many factors, including both biological and psychological components. Parents should know that depression does lift with time and with help. At times, mild depression can resolve on its own; however, this does not mean that one should take a wait-and-see attitude. The most important thing you can do as a parent if your child is depressed is to arrange for a professional evaluation, in order to access the most timely treatment and intervention. The sooner that depressed individuals can get professional assistance, the less disruption they will experience in significant areas of their lives, including their academic functioning.

If your child is down and having a bad day, speaking with you or a friend is probably all he or she needs. However, if your child's sad mood persists for more than two weeks and/or if he or she is getting out of his or her usual routine (for example, cutting classes, not seeing friends, not working out, not getting out of bed), it might be time for professional help. (See list of common triggers and symptoms of depression below.) Encourage your student to get help by going to the campus counseling center. If your child requires assistance beyond what the counseling center can provide, be assured that an appropriate referral will be made.

Many factors contribute to the onset of depression in college students, including biological predisposition, hormonal imbalances, negative thinking patterns, and a paucity of coping skills. Challenges to self-esteem and feelings of loss are common triggers for a depressive episode in college students. Some examples are:

- being overwhelmed by new academic and social demands
- break-up of a romantic relationship
- death of a family member or other loved one
- family problems/divorce
- decline in academic performance
- lack of emotional support from family or peers

Parents should be aware of the following symptoms of depression:

- depressed/sad mood most days
- tearfulness
- feelings of hopelessness and helplessness
- irritability and restlessness
- anhedonia—a loss of interest or pleasure in previously enjoyable activities
- sleep disturbance—difficulty falling or staying asleep, or excessive sleeping
- change in appetite, unintended weight gain or loss
- loss of energy, lethargy, fatigue
- difficulty with concentration or indecision
- feelings of guilt, worthlessness, and low self-esteem
- suicidal thoughts
- poor personal hygiene and appearance
- social isolation[2]

If your child displays signs of depression, encourage him or her to be honest about his or her feelings. Be a good listener and let your child speak freely. Listen with an open mind and do not minimize or deny their feelings. Also, offering simple solutions generally does not work. Saying things like "Just move on" or "Stop thinking about it" does not help alleviate the depression. No matter how much they would like to, people who are depressed can't just make themselves stop feeling that way.

Clinical depression is a serious condition that often impacts all aspects of an individual's ability to function. A person's mood, appetite, sleep, work, academic performance, and relationships may all be affected. Without effective treatment, individuals suffering from depression will often find that their symptoms worsen and continue for some time. The good news is that individuals who receive proper treatment often feel relief within weeks. If you are unsure about how to broach the subject of accessing professional help for your son or daughter, consult with the campus counseling center for suggestions about how to discuss this sensitive issue with your child.

Common treatments for depression include psychotherapy and medication. Research has shown that a combination of both psychotherapy and medication is often the most effective treatment. Medications prescribed for depression work on specific neural receptors in the brain to elevate or to stabilize mood. Common brand names include Prozac, Zoloft, Celexa, Lexapro, and Effexor. These medications have relatively few side effects and in general are very effective for alleviating depression within weeks.[3]

Suicidal Thoughts and Behaviors

No parents want to consider the possibility that their child may become so depressed and overwhelmed as to contemplate taking his or her own life. However, suicide is the second leading cause of death among college students (after accidents). People who are suicidal usually have underlying symptoms of depression and hopelessness. Their thinking can become so narrow that they see suicide as the only way to relieve their pain and solve their problems. They usually (but not always) give some warning sign before they take action. Parents should be aware that although females are more likely to make suicide attempts, males are more likely to actually take their own lives.

Parents should know the following warning signs and risk factors for suicide:

- directly threatening to hurt or kill himself or herself
- talking about having no reason to live; has no future-oriented thinking; cannot see things getting better
- talking or writing about death (including in text messages, away messages, academic writing assignments)
- social withdrawal and isolation
- history of suicide in family, extended family, or social network
- expressing the sensation of feeling trapped and having no way out
- someone significant in their lives has recently committed suicide
- putting affairs "in order"
- giving away personal possessions
- preoccupation with death
- access to firearms
- alcohol or drug use/abuse
- acting recklessly or engaging in dangerous/risky activities [4]

These symptoms must be taken very seriously. If your child is demonstrating one or more of the above behaviors, please seek help immediately. Contact a campus mental health professional or campus safety and security. In an immediate emergency, take your child to the nearest emergency room or call 911.

Self-Injury

A common, and often confusing, problem affecting university students involves self-injurious behavior. Self-mutilation, also called self-harm or self-injury, involves the deliberate, repetitive, and impulsive harming of one's body. It is usually done without the wish to commit suicide, and it is often an attempt to relieve tension or psychological pain. Types of self-injury can include cutting, burning, hair-pulling, scratching, picking at scabs, and hitting or punching oneself or objects.

Since the 1990s self-injury has become an increasing problem among adolescents and college students. Before the 1990s, self-injurious behavior was often considered to be a failed suicide attempt; however, professional opinion has changed, and this is no longer considered to be the case. Although self-injury is not considered a diagnosis in and of itself, it is recognized as a feature of an underlying mental health disorder.

As a parent, signs to look for include:

- unexplained frequent injuries (often cuts or burns)
- dressing inappropriately for the season to hide injuries
- feelings of low self-esteem
- easily becomes emotionally overwhelmed
- relationship problems
- difficulty functioning at school, home, or work

Self-injurious behavior typically begins during puberty and can last between five and ten years; however, without proper treatment these behaviors can last longer. Common experiences reported by self-injurers include feeling empty inside, difficulty expressing their feelings, loneliness, being misunderstood by others, and fearfulness of intimate relationships and adult responsibilities.

Self-injury is generally engaged in as a strategy for alleviating these negative feelings. This may be a hard concept to grasp and seems counterintuitive. However, cutting and other acts of self-harm release endorphins into the brain, which results in the person actually feeling relief from painful feelings. Often there is a repetitive cycle of self-injury that may be experienced as out of the person's control. Self-injurers may become hopeless and feel helpless about their lack of self-control and the addictive nature of their acts. This may, in turn, lead to actual suicide attempts.

Sometimes the self-injury may cause more harm than intended, which could result in medical complications or even death. For college students, there is particular concern about engaging in self-injurious behavior while intoxicated or under the influence of other substances. This is a significant factor in causing more serious injury than the individual may have intended.

Someone displaying self-injurious behavior is in great emotional pain and is using the behavior as a coping mechanism. These behaviors should not be minimized or ignored. The individual needs immediate treatment and should be seen by a professional with specific training and experience in treating self-injury. After an evaluation, a recommended course of treatment will be suggested to prevent the self-destructive cycle from continuing. Self-injury usually responds best to a combination of medication and psychotherapy.[5]

Trauma, Loss, and Grief Reactions

Events such as separation, death, illness, injury, or a job layoff can be described as significant losses. Grief is used to describe the emotions and experiences following a significant loss. It is common to feel intense sorrow, emptiness, longing, shock, anger, and/or helplessness after a significant loss. If the loss is unexpected or sudden, it is called a traumatic loss. There is no one way to properly experience, mourn, or deal with a loss. People have varied and unique ways of reacting and coping.

A traumatic event involves a negative incident that is out of one's ordinary experience. Some examples of a traumatic event include sexual assault, unexpected death of a loved one, mugging, physical assault, acts of terrorism, severe automobile accident, a life-threatening illness, a natural or man-made disaster. A traumatic event can also be experienced indirectly—for example, when a loved one has been the victim of a life-threatening event. Trauma can also occur by hearing about a traumatic event from someone else or by witnessing an extremely disturbing event.

Some possible emotional and physical reactions to a loss or to a traumatic event include the following:

- flashbacks of the event; intrusive, distressing thoughts about the event; or feelings that the event is reoccurring
- feeling very worried about safety for oneself and for loved ones
- feeling shock, numbness, detachment, and disbelief about the event
- feelings of depression, helplessness, and pervasive sadness
- an inability to identify feelings and general confusion
- difficulty with concentration and focusing on routine activities
- sleep disturbance that may include intense recurring nightmares
- exaggerated startle response
- avoiding people, places, or things that are reminders of the loss or trauma[6]

If your student has experienced a loss or trauma, encourage him or her to accept what he or she is feeling as being a normal reaction to an extreme situation. Let him or her know that intense feelings and out-of-character symptoms are understandable and to be expected, given the situation. Encourage your student to talk about it with you, other family members, friends, resident assistants, and other supportive individuals. Ignoring or minimizing their feelings will not alleviate them and can actually prolong a negative emotional reaction. In addition, the feelings can go underground, manifesting themselves problematically in other emotions such as anger and in inappropriate behavior. If you believe that speaking with friends and family is not sufficient, recommend that the student seek professional help. Counseling will help the student find words to express the feelings and will teach him or her strategies for coping. The counselor can also provide advocacy for a student who needs an extension of time on assignments or a leave of absence in order to fully recover.

It is important to give the student the time and space to heal. Whenever possible, this time should be somewhat structured so that individuals can continue at least some of their customary daily activities. They should be encouraged to use exercise, physical activity, and relaxation techniques to help get through the difficult time. If the trauma involves a loss, engaging in meaningful rituals related to the loss, such as creating a memorial service, lighting candles, leaving flowers, or other commemorative activities, can facilitate healing.

Most importantly, students should be encouraged to be gentle with themselves. They should not expect to function as if nothing has happened. Students may beat themselves up for not getting things done; however, they should remember that they are not lazy, they are grieving. Also remind them of coping strategies they have successfully used in the past to move through difficult times.

Parents should follow up with their student's resident assistant or the residence hall director to make sure their child is not withdrawing or isolating, and is staying connected to friends and helpers. Parents should also be on the lookout for signs such as loss of appetite, sleeplessness, or other physical symptoms that may signify the need for professional assistance.

Anger and Aggression

Anger is an emotion that everyone experiences at some point in life. At times, our anger is justified and can be healthy. For example, if we are being taken advantage of, anger can spur us on to take action (not necessarily aggressive) to correct the situation. At other times, if we lose control, anger can create problems in significant relationships, on the campus, in the residence hall, on the court or the playing field, or in the classroom.

Anger may be defined as an emotional reaction to injury or frustration. Often the frustration is related to feeling out of control or powerless; aggression is the resultant behavior used to express feelings of anger and/or frustration. It can include verbal attacks (insults, threats, cursing), a physical assault, or punishment. Not only is the individual targeted by the aggression hurt by the behavior, but negative consequences can also be experienced by the aggressive individual. These persons may experience loss of friendships and romantic relationships, legal problems, road rage, depression, substance abuse, and even removal from the campus. The enraged individual may also experience physical symptoms, such as hypertension, gastrointestinal problems, heart palpitations, and severe headaches.

If you believe that your student has a problem with anger and aggression, it is important that he or she get anger management counseling or other therapy to uncover the issues underlying the anger. Anger management goals include helping the student make a conscious decision to recognize and express anger in a way that does not hurt him or her or other individuals. It also teaches the student to recognize early warning signs of anger and to express it appropriately. Early warning signs of anger include:

- muscle tension, nervousness, sweating, racing heartbeat, and other physical symptoms of emotional arousal
- anxiety, irritability, distraction, restlessness, excessive preoccupation, and racing thoughts about the angering situation
- feeling keyed up or on edge, having emotional outbursts, and experiencing hypervigilance about further triggering events

Proper treatment will help your child realize that intense anger can be very dangerous. It will help him or her learn to verbalize emotions instead of acting on them. Expressing the emotions to a counselor may also lead to a change in perspective or interpretation of the events that were angering. This can help your child feel less preoccupied by anger, and prevent your child's acting in ways that he or she might regret later on.[7]

If you are concerned about how your child is handling his or her anger, remember that there are resources on most university campuses to help students understand and manage this problem. Students should not feel that they need to handle these issues by themselves. Encourage your child to use the counseling center—prior to engaging in behaviors that can jeopardize his or her college career, alienate peers, and lead to even more serious consequences.

Stress and Anxiety

Attending college is often accompanied by a variety of stressors, both social and academic, that can leave students feeling stressed and anxious. However, it is important for a parent to understand the difference between a simple stress reaction and a more enduring and at times debilitating anxiety disorder.

A stress reaction is usually triggered by some type of change. The degree of control we feel we have over a given change is inversely related to the amount of stress we experience. For example, getting stuck in a major traffic jam before an important meeting would most likely cause a great deal of stress for some of us, because the situation is clearly out of our control.

It should also be recognized that change can be positive or negative, and that both types produce stress. For students starting college, the change is a positive one, but it can nevertheless trigger stressful feelings. Common sources of stress for college students include:

- leaving family and friends at home
- commuting to school
- living with a roommate
- meeting new people
- problem solving on their own
- having less structure in their daily lives
- dealing with multiple priorities like completing schoolwork, making and maintaining friendships, working
- getting good grades
- meeting the expectations of parents, teachers, and friends
- time management issues
- being exposed to different values, cultures, lifestyles, and temptations

It is useful for parents and students to recognize the signs of stress, which can be physiological, behavioral, emotional, or cognitive:

- Physiological responses to stress are triggered by the sympathetic branch of the nervous system and can include heart racing, muscle tension, sweating, restlessness, and increased blood pressure. Chronic stress can lead to immune system deficiencies, frequent colds, a general lack of energy, and sleeping either too much or too little.
- Behavioral signals include nervous habits such as nail-biting (or other compulsive actions), overeating, angry outbursts and cursing, a change in habits (such as being more or less organized than usual), and a decrease in academic performance.
- Emotional signs may include anxiety, tearfulness, losing one's temper easily, chronic angry feelings, worry, irritability, and overreacting to minor events.
- Cognitive signs may include excessive preoccupation with a situation, repeatedly obsessing about an upsetting event, unstoppable negative and self-defeating thoughts, inability to concentrate, poor memory, and confusion.[8]

Stress reactions respond very well to relaxation techniques (see chapter 7). In addition, situational factors and circumstances can be planned for and altered to reduce stress. Unlike stress reactions, however, symptoms of an anxiety disorder are more debilitating and can interfere with a student's ability to function and meet responsibilities, such as the capacity to complete schoolwork, develop and maintain healthy relationships, attend classes, and go to work.

There are different types of anxiety disorders, which can only be accurately diagnosed by a mental health professional. However, familiarizing yourself with symptoms of common anxiety disorders will help you recognize if your child is moving beyond simple stress to an actual anxiety disorder.

Anxiety disorders include the following:

- Generalized anxiety disorder is characterized by an exaggerated, constant, overwhelming worry about basic everyday life events. Worry over routine events and their possible negative outcomes becomes the overriding thought and feeling pattern on the part of the individual. Physical symptoms can include muscle tension, trembling, headache, and nausea. When these symptoms last for a six-month period or longer, a diagnosis of general anxiety disorder may be given.
- Phobias are of two types: social or specific. Social phobia involves the intense fear of scrutiny in social situations. The person fears being humiliated and embarrassed and therefore avoids social interactions. This goes beyond shyness and may be a debilitating disorder that prevents students from participating in and enjoying basic social activities. Specific phobia involves the irrational fear of a specific thing or situation—for example, flying, elevators, or insects. Usually, the person begins to avoid situations in which he or she may be exposed to the feared object or situation.
- Panic disorder involves the repeated occurrence of "panic attacks"—brief, intense episodes of anxiety that include symptoms of dizziness, heart palpitations, shortness of breath, sweating, abdominal distress, chest pain, and fear of dying.
- Posttraumatic stress disorder (PTSD) may occur after witnessing or experiencing a traumatic event, such as an accident, rape, a terrorist attack, physical abuse, a natural disaster, or the sudden and unexpected loss of a loved one. Symptoms include intrusive and unwanted thoughts about the event, nightmares, flashbacks, depression, and difficulty with concentration.
- Obsessive-compulsive disorder (OCD) may involve both repeated thoughts (obsessions) and actions (compulsions). These thoughts and behaviors are experienced as out of control and irrational by the person experiencing them; yet they have no ability to stop them. For example, a common obsession might be the worry about being contaminated by germs, and the related compulsion may be to repeatedly wash one's hands.[9]

Although each anxiety disorder has specific symptoms, there is a common thread of irrational, excessive worry and fear that connects them. They can often be debilitating and will not resolve without proper evaluation and treatment. Common treatment modalities for anxiety disorders include psychotherapy (cognitive behavioral treatments are proven to be very effective) as well as medication. Often certain classes of antidepressants are prescribed to treat anxiety disorders, as well as antianxiety medications. However, many antianxiety medications (but not all) can become addictive. Therefore, if your student is prescribed one of these drugs, he or she should be made aware of this risk and be followed closely by a psychiatrist. The student should also be made aware that antianxiety medications should never be combined with alcohol.[10]

Schizophrenia

Far less common than depression and anxiety disorders, schizophrenia is a complicated disorder that often first presents itself in college-age students. It involves various disturbances in an individual's thinking patterns, perceptual abilities, and social skills. Parents should know that individuals with schizophrenia often experience odd or bizarre thoughts and perceptions that are out of touch with reality (psychosis). For example, the person will have delusional thoughts and hear voices or see things that are not there—that is, have auditory or visual hallucinations. The person also will demonstrate various cognitive and behavioral changes, including extreme social withdrawal and lack of emotional expression. This constellation of symptoms will cause marked impairment in the individual's academic, social, and occupational functioning.[11]

Schizophrenia is usually diagnosed when the person has a first "psychotic break"; however, other symptoms such as delusional thoughts, cognitive difficulties, and social withdrawal may be present even earlier. Schizophrenia may have a sudden onset, or it may develop gradually for years. It is a serious disorder that needs psychiatric evaluation and treatment. There is some evidence to suggest that that the sooner diagnosis and treatment occur, the better the prognosis for the person. With this is mind, if parents notice changes in their child's mood, thinking process, academic performance, and behaviors (especially social withdrawal and bizarre behavior), they should encourage him or her to be evaluated as soon as possible.

Treatment for schizophrenia usually includes medication and supportive psychotherapy. Common antipsychotic medications prescribed include Abilify, Seroquel, Risperdal, Zyprexa, and Haldol. These are powerful medications with potentially serious side effects and must be monitored closely by a psychiatrist.[12]

Bipolar Disorder

Bipolar disorder, or manic depression, is a disorder that most often causes extreme shifts in a person's mood and energy level, from feeling hypermanic to very depressed. More than ten million people in the United States are diagnosed with bipolar disorder. Episodes of mania and depression vary from person to person, but they may last from days to months. Symptoms of depression have been previously discussed. Symptoms of mania (or a manic state) include:

- an excessively elated or an extremely angry/irritable mood
- a dramatic increase in energy level and an extreme reduction in the need for sleep
- racing thoughts
- an increase in talking and a rapid rate of speech
- grandiosity
- impulsive, risky behaviors without an awareness of possible consequences

Many of these symptoms, when present at elevated levels, can lead to psychotic thinking and extremely dangerous behaviors.[13]

Treatment for bipolar disorder must include medication and often psychotherapy. Common medications include the use of mood stabilizers such as lithium and Depakote. Mood stabilizers need to be monitored by a psychiatrist, and many patients will need to have ongoing blood work in order to monitor therapeutic levels of the medication, possible toxicity, and other side effects. Although this is a serious illness, with proper evaluation and care, bipolar disorder is very treatable.[14]

Eating Disorders

Individuals who suffer with eating disorders spend a great deal of their time obsessing about food, their weight, and their body image. They are often preoccupied with counting and recounting the calories they consume. They may weigh themselves frequently each day and go on extremely restrictive diets. Persons with eating disorders complain of "feeling fat" even if their weight is normal or below normal. They may feel guilty after eating and/or feel worried about gaining weight even after eating a small portion of food. Often they see foods as "good" or "bad" and base their self-esteem on how well they can control what they eat. In some cases, they may see eating at all as a defeat of their willpower.

Unfortunately, in our society we are bombarded with media images of "perfect bodies" on a daily basis. One of the many negative results is the development of unrealistic standards for beauty and thinness, and obsession with body image. For people with eating disorders, thinner is always better.

Successful weight control becomes intricately tied to their self-image and self-esteem.

Having an eating disorder often involves a vicious cycle of repeated, ritualistic, and rigid behavior focused on food. It can reach dangerous, life-threatening proportions and require not only psychological intervention, but medical attention as well. Common eating disorders include anorexia nervosa, bulimia nervosa, and binge eating/compulsive overeating, each of which will be discussed in turn.

Anorexia nervosa is a dangerous illness that involves using self-starvation to lose weight. Anorexics are obsessively afraid of being fat. Often their self-perception is so distorted that they continue to believe they are fat, even when their body weight is dangerously below the normal range. Genetic and emotional factors contribute to the development of anorexia. A typical patient profile is a high-achieving female from a middle-class or upper-middle-class family who values appearance, control, and perfection. The individual is usually a good student and compliant with parental and social expectations. Parents may directly or indirectly communicate a value for thinness and a disdain for "overeating" or for indulging in particular foods, which can inadvertently facilitate the development of anorexia.

Common symptoms of anorexia include failing to maintain a normal, healthy body weight, digestive problems and constipation, dry skin, dry hair, cold hands and feet, general weakness, sleep disturbance, and amenorrhea (loss of menstrual periods). More severe problems may develop as weight loss progresses, such as a weakened immune system, ketosis (severe chemical imbalances), stress fractures, and cardiac problems, which can be fatal.

Bulimia nervosa is a disorder that involves recurrent episodes of binge eating, which are then followed by purging. The purging is usually done by self-induced vomiting, abusing laxatives and diuretics, starving, or excessive exercising. Bulimics are subject to a variety of medical problems caused by their eating and purging habits. Often bulimics are difficult to identify because they are usually of average or slightly above average weight. They are secretive about bingeing and purging and most often do it in private. They may have rapid weight gains and losses and medical problems, which can include dry skin, dehydration, constipation and other digestive disorders, kidney damage, inflammation of the esophagus, dental problems, and dangerous electrolyte imbalances, which can lead to life-threatening heart irregularities and even coma or death.

Binge eating or compulsive overeating is a disorder in which the person suffers from episodes of uncontrollable overeating (bingeing) followed by feelings of extreme guilt and depression. The person may eat large amounts of food rapidly and in a pressured fashion. Often they will continue eating after they feel full and even uncomfortable. They may not eat in front of others and are usually ashamed of their eating behaviors. They frequently eat alone or in private. Persons with binge-eating disorder are usually overweight and may become obese. As their weight increases, they may begin to suffer from shortness of breath, high blood pressure, and joint problems. If they become severely obese, their problems can progress to osteoarthritis and life-threatening disorders, such as heart disease, gall bladder disease, and diabetes.

There are many complicated reasons, both psychological and biological, for a person to develop an eating disorder. The treatments vary depending on the disorder and the individual. It is most important that parents become aware of the symptoms and be able to offer appropriate assistance if necessary. Eating disorders should not be ignored or minimized, as they are an outward demonstration of emotional distress, as well as medically debilitating. Often there is a co-morbid psychological disorder (such as depression) present in persons diagnosed with an eating disorder. If you suspect that your child is struggling with an eating disorder, your goal should be to ensure that he or she us medically stable and receiving counseling specific to eating disorders. Treatments will include psychotherapy and, at times, medication. For individuals with anorexia, highly specialized treatment is necessary, and this may take place in an inpatient facility.[15]

In terms of prevention, parents are urged to examine their own attitudes toward food, weight, and body image. Parents who make disparaging remarks about their own weight and size may inadvertently encourage a negative self-image in their children. Similarly, commenting on how much their child is eating or asking "Do you really need to eat that doughnut?" sends a message that eating for enjoyment or pleasure is not acceptable. Parents are encouraged to help their children challenge the constant messages that bombard them about the importance of thinness and striving for physical perfection.

Troubled and Dangerous Students

Recent media coverage has raised awareness about events on college campuses that involve troubled and violent students.[16] Often friends, family, roommates, classmates, and acquaintances of troubled students are made aware of their disturbance or of the potentially dangerous or self-destructive situation before it happens. However, individuals may be uncertain about which kinds of warning signs to take seriously and/or whether reporting these signs to an authority is the appropriate thing to do. Therefore we are offering a list of possible warning signs that parents and students should always take seriously. We also encourage parents and students to disclose their concerns to campus personnel, such as the counseling center staff, residential life, student affairs, and campus safety and security. Students can also inform the students of concern or threat assessment team on the campus.

Warning signs for troubled and dangerous students include:

- Making direct statements about the intention to harm himself or herself and/or other members of the college community.
- Making statements that hint at the intention to do harm to self or others, for example, "This might be the last time you see me" or "If I were you, I'd stay out of the library tomorrow."
- Demonstrating an extreme difficulty in adjusting to college life. These students are often isolated, depressed, or very angry with campus staff or peers.
- Significant behavioral changes and/or changes in the person's appearance, habits, or mood.
- Disruptive behavior in the classroom and in the residence hall.
- The student makes statements about having access to firearms or other weapons.
- The student is preoccupied by violence in general and/or by previous violent events in schools or colleges.

If your child is demonstrating any of the above behaviors, you should address it directly and consider contacting campus personnel such as counseling center staff, residential life, and campus safety and security for assistance. Do not minimize these behaviors. Above all, have your child psychiatrically evaluated and make sure that he or she follows the resultant recommendations for treatment. At times, this may include hospitalization, which you may find very painful as a parent. However, this may be needed to ensure the safety of your child and/or other members of the campus community. Certainly, inpatient treatment is preferable to your child's acting out in ways that are dangerous and life altering. As with other concerns, parents can always consult with the counseling center about how to approach this difficult topic with their son or daughter.

CHEMICAL DEPENDENCY AND ADDICTIVE BEHAVIORS

Alcohol Abuse and Dependency

Many students begin using alcohol and drugs during high school and continue this behavior in college. For other students, college will provide the freedom and distance from parental control for them to begin experimenting with the use of substances. College students often give the following reasons for using alcohol and other substances:

- to celebrate special occasions
- to feel more comfortable in social situations
- because many of their peers use alcohol and other drugs as an integral part of their social life
- to relieve emotions such as anxiety, stress, anger, sadness, loneliness, and fear

The use of alcohol and substances usually begins as something fun and recreational; however, with sustained use, it can develop into problematic behavior affecting many areas of the student's life. Parents need to know how to speak to their children about alcohol and other drugs and to recognize when a problem might be developing.

Unlike other drugs, alcohol is legal, and drinking is considered a socially acceptable behavior in most of society. It is easy to obtain, and students often have ready access to bars and clubs near campus. Troubled drinkers will exhibit certain symptoms that separate them from social drinkers. Most will demonstrate:

- A preoccupation with getting intoxicated.
- Increased tolerance; over time, the individual needs more and more alcohol to get the same effect.
- Drinking alone; the person will drink when no one else is drinking and will drink in isolation and sometimes in secrecy.
- Using alcohol as a medication, for example to reduce anxiety or depression. Substance abusers often use alcohol as a tranquilizer or sometimes as a nightcap to induce sleep. In these cases, an underlying anxiety disorder may be fueling the substance abuse problem.
- Consuming drinks quickly so that the alcohol will act rapidly upon the body.
- Blacking out, which involves memory impairment such that the drinker has difficulty recalling events surrounding the drinking episode.
- Maintaining a supply; problem drinkers feel safer and more comfortable knowing that alcohol is always readily available.
- Problems in academic, occupational, or interpersonal function; the person's level of alcohol consumption is causing him or her to miss classes or work, to perform poorly, and/or to create serious conflict in friendships or romantic relationships.
- Loss of control; the drinker often ends up drinking more than he or she had intended.

- Denial; although others can readily see the problems in functioning that the individual is experiencing and have witnessed repeated incidents of intoxication, blackouts, and impairment, the alcohol-dependent individual continues to deny that this is a problem.

As an individual continues to use alcohol on a regular basis, abuse of the drug can turn into dependence, such that the drinker will display an inability to control the frequency and amount of alcohol consumed. Often drinking will escalate despite the individual's knowledge of the negative consequences and effects. The problem drinker may develop a tolerance so strong that he or she can longer feel intoxicated no matter how many drinks have been consumed. At this level of abuse and dependence, the drinker may no longer be able to function without drinking. If the drinker stops drinking, withdrawal symptoms will begin.

Physical symptoms of intoxication include a staggered gait, lack of muscle coordination, eye abnormalities, and slurred speech. Problem drinkers often demonstrate patterns of frequent hangovers, nausea, and even malnutrition. They may eventually become less and less concerned with grooming, and their physical appearance may deteriorate.

Problem drinkers may be suffering from an underlying depression or other mood disturbance. They are unable to use healthy coping skills, and therefore they use alcohol to deal with stress, anger, boredom, and social anxiety. As their drinking problem increases, they may show signs of dramatic mood swings and intense anxiety or anger. They may even feel guilty and regretful about their behavior in the immediate aftermath of a drinking episode, but still be unable to stop. Significantly, denial of the seriousness of the particular drinking incident, or of problematic drinking in general, also undercuts the individual's motivation to change his or her behavior.

Alcohol abuse and dependence also affects the brain and impairs cognition. Often a student abusing alcohol will perform poorly in school. The drinker may report decreased attention, decreased concentration span, and difficulties with memory, all skills needed for academic success. In addition, the drinker will often use poor judgment and demonstrate decreased decision-making ability. As the addiction progresses, blackouts become more frequent and problematic, and the drinker's overall mental state deteriorates.

Over time, relationships with friends and family will also begin to deteriorate. Drinking becomes the most important thing in the drinker's life, and other things and people become secondary. Often, due to a variety of factors (increased spending on alcohol, poor judgment, loss of job), the drinker will develop financial problems. In addition, other problematic behaviors may involve legal issues, traffic violations, violent behavior, vandalism, and unplanned and unwanted sexual experiences, including being the victim or perpetrator of sexual assault.[17]

The majority of college students are underage and, by definition, cannot legally purchase or drink alcohol. However, because alcohol is nevertheless readily available, parents are encouraged to talk to their student about alcohol and substance abuse on campus prior to his or her arriving at school. Without passing judgment or accusing, let your student know that you are aware of how common substance use and abuse are in the new environment, and that this is an issue that he or she will inevitably encounter and need to make wise decisions about.

Parents should also be aware that there is a genetic predisposition toward abusing alcohol (and other substances). Therefore if a family member, including a parent, grandparent, sibling, aunt, or uncle, has a history of alcohol (or other substance) dependency, students should know that they are at greater risk for developing this problem. Parents should urge their at-risk children to be especially cautious about alcohol use and honest about any sense they have of losing control and becoming dependent.

On many college campuses, abstinence is not seen as a particularly realistic goal. Instead, alcohol and other drugs (AOD) education and prevention programs focus on harm reduction. To that end, students are offered the following guidelines:

- Do not drink more than three times per week.
- Do not drink within six to eight hours before driving a car, working, or going to class.
- Do not consume more than one drink in a sixty-minute period.
- Do not binge drink, which can be defined as drinking five or more drinks (four drinks for women) on any occasion.

Students should also be educated about avoiding the use of instruments and techniques designed to increase consumption of alcohol in shorter periods of time, such as funnels, "shotgunning" beers, keg stands, and so on. The body is ill equipped to deal with large amounts of alcohol in short periods of time, and what may seem like a fun new thing to try can often end up as a trip to the hospital or worse. Often, binge drinking and using techniques to increase consumption take place during drinking games frequently engaged in by college students, such as Beer Pong.

Many students do not understand that drinking large amounts of alcohol can lead to lethal consequences. Alcohol is a depressant, and, as such, slows breathing and heart rate and causes blood pressure to fall. When blood alcohol levels go up too quickly in a short period of time, alcohol poisoning can rapidly set in. When that happens, the areas of the brain responsible for maintaining breathing, heart rate, and blood pressure literally stop functioning. People then lose consciousness, and they can die. Another life-threatening occurrence during alcohol poisoning is death from choking on one's own vomit. As mentioned earlier, parents should be aware that more than eighteen hundred college students die each year from alcohol poisoning or related accidents.[18]

Parents should know that in recent years, beverages that combine alcohol with large amounts of caffeine have become available. These beverages target high school and college-aged individuals, and, in fact, this cohort has been found to extensively indulge in the use of these products. Although some, such as Four Loko (also called "Blackout in a Can"), have been banned in some states, they remain available on the Internet.[19] Young people also combine caffeinated beverages such as Red Bull with alcohol to achieve the same effect.

In addition to awareness about the rampant use of alcoholic (and combined alcohol and caffeine) beverages on the campus, parents should engage in an ongoing dialogue with their student regarding their expectations around drinking behavior.

Other Substances and Abuse

Alcohol is not the only substance your student will have access to while at college. The following is a list of common drugs that often find their way onto the college campus. It is useful for parents and caregivers to know the most popular drugs available on campus, how they are taken, what the long- and short-term side effects are, and the common street names for these drugs.

Legal/Prescription Drugs

For most college students, alcohol remains the number one drug of choice; however, prescription drug abuse is increasingly prevalent on the university campus. Many students unfortunately believe that using and abusing "smart" drugs is not harmful. Students may believe that because these drugs are made in regulated laboratories, they are safe to take without medical supervision. Parents need to know that prescription medication is second only to marijuana for abused drugs in the United States. Prescription drugs are usually easy for students to obtain. Many online pharmacies do not require prescriptions, and students may fake medical conditions or learning disabilities in order to get a prescription from a doctor. Most commonly, students steal from or are given prescription drugs by family members, friends, or acquaintances who have valid prescriptions.[20]

Common prescription drugs that students are most likely to abuse include the following:

- Opioids/painkillers, such as OxyContin, OxyCodoen, and Vicodin. These narcotic pain relievers are the most abused class of drugs among Americans aged twelve and over. These drugs may cause feelings of hap-

piness, euphoria, and being "high"; such effects are enhanced when the drugs are taken in combination with alcohol. The pills are often crushed to break down the time-release coating. In this way, larger amounts of the drug are released at once and its effects are increased. Common street names include Oxy, O.C., and Cotton.[21]
- Central nervous system (CNS) depressants like Valium and Xanax, usually prescribed to treat anxiety and insomnia. These drugs may be abused by students when they want to relax, get some sleep, or come down from feeling high. Common street names include Vikes and Norco.[22]
- Stimulants, including Ritalin, Adderall, Concerta, and Dexedrine, which have a paradoxically calming effect when used as prescribed to treat patients with attention deficit hyperactivity disorder (ADHD). On campus, students frequently abuse stimulants to increase energy, alertness, concentration, and attention. Students may use the drugs as study aids or may abuse them to control appetite, lose weight, stay up late, or elicit feelings of euphoria. According to research studies, 25 percent of college students have abused stimulants, often in an attempt to improve their grades and to remain academically competitive with their classmates, who may also be abusing stimulants. Students take the pills whole, chew them, inject or snort the crushed powder to achieve a quicker high, and they often take them in combination with alcohol. Common street names include Jif, Skippy, Vitamin R, and R-Ball.[23]

All medications have side effects, and therefore the use of these types of prescription drugs needs to be managed by a doctor. When these drugs are taken with alcohol or combined with other drugs, the risk of dangerous side effects rises exponentially. As with illegal drugs, abusing painkillers, CNS depressants, and stimulants over time produces a tolerance to the drugs. This means that more of the drug will need to be consumed in order to achieve the same effect. Physical withdrawal symptoms may be experienced if the user stops taking the drugs. Students should be made aware that taking large doses of prescription painkillers or CNS depressants or mixing them with other substances puts them at risk for respiratory depression and death. Although stimulants are not as physically addictive, they can lead to psychological dependence. Students may experience paranoia, angry outbursts, increased body temperature, seizures, heart failure, and even death when these drugs are taken in high doses.

It is important to remember that many students have valid medical reasons for taking prescription drugs, and abuse prevention efforts should not stigmatize these individuals. However, if your son or daughter does *not* have a valid reason for taking these medications, you can help minimize the risk for abuse by building awareness about potential dangers and making your own expectations clear.

Illegal Drugs

Parents should also be aware of the illegal drugs that college students can access with relative ease. They include the following:[24] :

- Marijuana/cannabis is a plant that contains THC, a chemical that alters perception. Common street names include pot, weed, herb, MJ, and the Kind. Marijuana is smoked in a cigarette (joint, doobee, fatty, jay), in a water pipe (bong), in a cigarette-sized hollow metal tube called a bat, and even baked into brownies. In the short term, it may give a feeling of relaxation and disconnection from reality, and it can make ordinary things seem significant or amusing. For some users, it can also invoke paranoid feelings and anxiety. Long-term effects of marijuana use include psychological addiction, memory loss, shortened attention span, apathy, weight gain, breathing problems, colds, heart palpitations, gynecomastia (male breast growth), and smoking-related cancers.
- Cocaine is a white or yellowish powder extracted from the cocoa plant. It is a stimulant and often cut (mixed) with other white substances (aspirin, caffeine pills, and even Ajax) to make the quantity appear larger before it is sold. Street names include coke, blow, snow, toot, blanco, or chocha. Cocaine is snorted in lines, generally off a surface like a mirror, with a cut straw or money rolled into the form of a straw. It can also be smoked (freebasing), combined into a marijuana cigarette and smoked (dirty joint or C-Joint), rubbed on to the gums (freeze), and even dissolved in water and injected. In the short term it increases energy, makes the heart beat faster, and gives the sense of mental acuity for the duration of the high, which can vary greatly depending on the dose, the method used, and the frequency. Afterward, the user may feel fatigue, insomnia from increased heart rate, and extreme congestion. Long-term use can lead to addiction, destruction of the nasal passages (if snorted), lung damage (if smoked), paranoia, aggression, depression, heart attack, and death.
- Ecstasy is a chemical substance that combines methamphetamines with hallucinogens. It is a stimulant with a perceptual altering component. Common street names include MDMA, XTC, E-bombs, or E. Ecstasy is taken in tablet, capsule, or powder form, and it can be packaged to look like prescription drugs. In the short term it produces the feeling of alertness and euphoria; however, at high doses it can cause jitteriness. Some users experience a state of empathy and feelings of closeness with others, often accompanied by lowered inhibitions. Ecstasy increases heart rate, body temperature, and blood pressure. Its effects can last up to twenty-four hours, but usually averages three to four hours per dose. Long-term use can lead to chronic muscle tension, involuntary teeth clenching, nau-

sea, blurred vision, rapid eye movement, faintness, chills and sweating, depression, sleep problems, severe anxiety, and paranoia.
- Psilocybin mushroom is a hallucinogen that often comes in a dried mushroom form. Common street names are magic mushrooms, shrooms, caps, and stems. Psilocybin mushrooms are generally taken orally and ingested or can even be made into a tea. In the short term the effects are similar to that of LSD and often depend on the user's mood and environment. These effects may include relaxation and euphoria, and at higher doses may include hallucinations with distortions of color and/or sound. Other short-term effects can be extreme anxiety, fear, and paranoia. Short-term physical effects may include nausea, vomiting, and muscle weakness. Depending on dosage these effects can last anywhere from two to eight hours.
- Methamphetamine is an addictive stimulant. It is a crystal powder that is usually white or yellow (depending on the purity), and it also comes in rock form. Common street names include crystal meth, bling bling, glass, and ice. Methamphetamine can be snorted, smoked, swallowed, or injected. In the short term, depending on how it is taken, the user experiences increased activity level, suppressed appetite, "a rush of well-being" when smoked or injected, and a "high" when snorted or swallowed. Tolerance develops quickly, and users need more meth to get the same level of high, forcing the user to go on binges that can last for days. Long-term users can experience depression, anxiety, fatigue, paranoia, aggression insomnia, hallucinations (especially the sensation of their skin crawling), delusions, and sometimes suicidal or homicidal thoughts.
- Heroin is an opiate narcotic that comes from morphine, which is produced from poppy seeds. Heroin is a bitter-tasting white to dark brown powder. Street names include dope, smack, junk, Big H, and horse. Heroin can be snorted, smoked, or injected. In recent years, the high quality of heroin available has made it easier to snort; therefore, people such as college students who previously may have been put off by the need to shoot up can now easily experiment with heroin by snorting. This has led to a significant increase in the number of people experimenting with heroin and becoming addicted. Heroin initially elicits a feeling of euphoria and limits the body's perception of pain. Heroin is highly addictive, with some users reporting that they were hooked after one experience. Other long-term effects include infection of the heart lining, liver disease, complications from shooting up (HIV/AIDS, Hepatitis C). Withdrawal symptoms include diarrhea, vomiting, cold flashes with chills, uncontrollable muscle contractions, insomnia, and muscle and bone pain. Withdrawal can begin within a few hours after the last use, peaks between two and three days, and can last up to a week.
- LSD is a hallucinogen that usually comes in colored tablets, blotter paper, clear liquid, or squares of gelatin. Common street names include acid,

brown bombers, dots, electric Kool-Aid, and sugar cubes. It is generally taken orally, but droplets of liquid or gelatin can even be inserted into the eyes. Depending on the amount taken and the user's mood, in the short term, users experience increased heart rate and blood pressure, feeling many emotions all at once or in quick succession, as well as delusions and hallucinations. Long-term effects may include flashback experiences that occur days or even years after the LSD use.
- PCP is an anesthetic drug that comes in the form of a tan to brown powder or gummy substance, as well as tablets and capsules. Common street names are Angel Dust and Hog. It is often added to other drugs such as marijuana, LSD, or methamphetamine; therefore, it is often taken inadvertently. PCP can be smoked, snorted, swallowed, or injected. Short-term effects include feelings similar to alcohol intoxication, hallucinations, anxiety, disorientation, paranoia, and violent behavior. PCP inflicts permanent damage on the brain. Long-term side effects include memory loss, depression, loss of motor skills, and weight loss.
- Steroids are manufactured, testosterone-like drugs. Common street names are juice, roids, arnies, gym candy, balls, and bulls. Steroids come in tablets or liquid form and can be taken orally or injected. They are often taken in patterns called "cycling," such that they are taken over a specific period of time, then stopped and started again, so that continuous use is avoided. Short-term effects of steroids include increased muscle mass, strength, and endurance; however, they can also cause liver tumors, jaundice, water retention, and high blood pressure. Some users show aggression and poor judgment because they feel invincible. Long-term side effects include hypertension, high cholesterol, stunted growth, and heart damage. Women who use steroids experience an irreversible deepening of the voice and masculinization of genitalia, while men experience shrinking of testicles and impotence.
- "Bath Salts" is a relative newcomer to the drug scene, with critical numbers of negative reports to poison control centers noted beginning in 2011. A synthetic derivative of cathenine, a plant grown in Africa, Bath Salts has been banned in New Jersey, and other states are rapidly following suit. Not to be confused with Epson salts or other actual bath products, these potentially dangerous drugs have been sold at gas stations, mini-marts, and head shops under such brand names as "Ivory Wave," "Blue Wave," "Red Dove," and "Vanilla Sky." Reputedly used primarily by adolescents and young adults, Bath Salts produces a high similar to methamphetamine and hallucinogenic effects similar to LSD. It has been reported to produce negative side effects such as paranoia, violent behavior, serious self-injury, suicidality, psychosis, and dangerously rapid heartbeat. A substance that can be snorted, injected, or smoked, Bath Salts is being viewed as an

emerging health threat by poison control centers and has been implicated in several violent crimes.[25]
- "Spice"/"K2" is another relative newcomer to the drug scene. It is considered to be a synthetic form of marijuana, consisting of a mixture of herbs that have been sprayed with chemical substances that are potentially far more dangerous than actual marijuana. Like Bath Salts, Spice/K2 has been readily available in head shops, tobacco shops, and convenience stores. The most frequent consumers of these substances are fourteen- to twenty-seven-year olds. Spice/K2 produces a high far more intense than marijuana and has been reported to cause hallucinations, seizures, coma, elevated blood pressure, disorientation, and panic attacks. Because of hundreds of reports by emergency room physicians regarding the serious side effects they have noted, several states have banned the sale of these products. In 2011, the U.S. Drug Enforcement Administration (DEA) made Spice/K2 a "Schedule 1 drug," similar to nonsynthetic marijuana, LSD, Ecstasy, and heroin. Spice/K2 is usually sold in foil packets under additional names such as Spice Gold, Spice Silver, Skunk, and Yucatan Fire and is smoked to produce a high.[26]

Signs of Substance Abuse

Parents often wonder how they can tell if their child is abusing substances. Below you will find a list of some common signs of substance abuse that parents should be aware of:

- Drinking and/or drugging to calm nerves, forget worries, or boost a depressed/sad mood.
- Missing morning classes, falling behind on course work, and sudden or incremental deterioration in academic performance.
- Guilt about drinking and/or drugging.
- Unsuccessful attempts to cut down or stop drinking and/or drugging.
- Experiencing unwanted consequences and acting irresponsibly, such as getting in trouble with school and/or legal authorities, fighting, destruction of property, or frequent hangovers.
- Lying about or hiding drinking and/or drugging habits.
- Causing harm to oneself or someone else as a result of drinking and/or drugging.
- Needing to drink and/or drug in increasingly greater amounts in order to achieve desired effect.
- Feeling irritable, resentful, unreasonable, and moody when not drinking and/or drugging.
- Medical, social, family, or financial problems have led to using alcohol and/or drugs as a coping mechanism.

- Spending a great deal of time getting and using alcohol and/or drugs.
- Drinking and/or drugging in risky situations such as before driving or before engaging in unwanted/unprotected sex.
- Social life revolves entirely around drinking and/or drugging, and there is a loss of interest in other activities that used to be pleasurable.

GUIDELINES FOR PARENTS REGARDING SUBSTANCE ABUSE

- Parents should not wait or avoid talking about their suspicions with their student. Choose a good time to talk with your child, for example, soon after an alcohol-and/or drug-related problem has occurred. Avoid confronting or speaking with someone who is actively under the influence of alcohol or drugs. Choose a time when he or she is not intoxicated and when both of you are calm. Make sure that you can speak privately. It is crucial during this time to be an active listener, while maintaining a nonjudgmental stance toward your son or daughter as a person.
- Let your child know that you are genuinely concerned about his or her drinking and/or drugging. Back up your concern with examples of the ways in which his or her drinking and/or drugging has caused problems for both of you, including the most recent incident. *Expect resistance and denial of the problem*; this is part of the disorder. However, it is important that you continue to let your child know that you love and care for him or her and that you want to be supportive in *getting your child help*.
- Don't minimize or make excuses for your child's behavior. Many parents try to protect their student from the consequences of his or her drinking and/or drugging behavior by making excuses, rationalizing, or ignoring the problem behavior. Denying and minimizing allow your child to continue abusing substances and avoid changing his or her behavior. It will make the situation worse and delay recovery.
- Let your child know that risky drinking, including binge drinking, and/or drug use, can lead to more severe problems including alcohol dependence (alcoholism) and/or drug dependence, as well as to injuries to themselves or others, unwanted/unprotected sex, academic failure, and interpersonal problems.
- Seek out resources on campus to help your child. Many universities have an alcohol and other drug (AOD) office dedicated to helping substance-abusing students. You can also ask the counseling center staff what resources are available for your child and how to motivate him or her to use them. If the staff of AOD services or the counseling center ascertains that your son or daughter needs more specialized or intensive treatment than they can provide on campus, they will inform you about appropriate off-campus resources.

- Do what you can to encourage your child to use the resources you identify, but remember that the only person who can ultimately take action and make a change is your child. Nevertheless, as a parent, you should be *persistent* in urging your child to seek help. Chemical dependency is an example of a problem in which a parent *must be* actively and consistently involved in the service of accessing appropriate treatment.

GAMBLING ADDICTION AND COMPULSIVE GAMING

Many parents are surprised to find out that gambling is becoming a significant problem across university campuses. In general, more attention and outreach on campus is usually given to alcohol and drug addiction, but gambling addiction is a rising concern. Gambling addictions are generally easier to hide than substance addictions, and with the Internet making online gambling readily available, students run the risk of becoming hooked while sitting in their dorm room.

Many students wager on sporting events, but many more are addicted to video games and online gambling. Students can get addicted to the rush provided by video games, and this easily transfers to video poker and then online poker machines. Some students can spend large quantities of time and money on these games.[27]

Parents should talk to their students about the dangers of gambling and be aware of symptoms such as:

- lying about gambling to family and friends
- frequently borrowing money to gamble
- neglecting responsibilities due to gambling
- frequent mood swings that coincide with winning or losing
- gambling to escape problems
- relationship conflicts, often centered around money
- stealing to pay for gambling
- using tuition or scholarship funds to gamble
- unsuccessfully trying to cut back on gambling
- gambling to "chase" (recoup) lost money[28]

If you think that your student might have a gambling addiction, talk to him or her using the same techniques that were described earlier in this chapter for substance abuse.

Parents should also be aware that students can become addicted to online gaming without developing a gambling problem. Students may feel compelled to spend inordinate amounts of time and resources playing complex online games, squandering large sums of money, as well as time better spent studying, socializing, or participating in healthier activities. Addiction to online games can therefore lead to poor academic performance, social isolation, and financial problems. Parents should be alert to their child spending all of his or her free time on the computer and showing little or no interest in participating in other activities. Excessive and compulsive preoccupation with online gaming should not be viewed as harmless. If your child feels compelled to participate in these games (or in a particular game), professional assistance may be in order.

ADDITIONAL RECOMMENDATIONS FOR PARENTS

Perhaps during a phone conversation or visit home, a parent may be able to detect an emotional or addiction problem that might need to be addressed before it escalates into something even more serious. We are not suggesting that parents act as trained mental health providers, attempting to make diagnoses and prescribe treatment. However, with an increased awareness of common disorders, parents may be better able to help recognize the presence of psychological distress or possible addiction in a student. Awareness of the signs and symptoms of psychological and addictive disorders, coupled with good communication skills, will go a long way in helping parents provide support for their child.

It is important to remember that while e-mails and text messages are common modes of maintaining contact between parent and child and may provide useful information and possible clues about emotional disturbance, this faster, more convenient, and now more popular communication method should not be a replacement for talking on the phone or seeing your child in person. Direct personal communication and contact can often provide the most accurate overall picture of how well your student is functioning.

In a campus environment, where the prevalence of psychological disturbance and addictive behavior is increasing and services to help students may be limited, parents can prove to be the most important resource in helping students recognize problems that may require evaluation and treatment. With proper assessment, treatment, and follow-up, many psychological disorders and addictive behaviors can be successfully treated.

As counseling professionals with years of clinical experience, we strongly believe that students need to be evaluated by trained mental health professionals. These include psychologists, clinical social workers, mental health counselors, addiction specialists, psychiatrists, and psychiatric nurse practitioners.

Psychiatrists are medical doctors who have expertise in the treatment of psychological disorders and the use of specific medications to treat these disorders. All too often, students are given prescriptions for psychoactive medications by their family doctor. This may be done for a variety of reasons, including comfort level with the doctor (as the student usually knows the family physician), ease and convenience of reaching out to an established contact, and avoidance of the stigma sometimes attached to a psychiatric diagnosis.

Although many family practitioners, internists, and general practitioners are well intentioned in their treatment of patients with psychiatric symptoms, they have not received the same level of training in mental health problems as a psychiatrist, and as a result, they do not have the same level of expertise in prescribing psychoactive medications or understanding the necessity for related psychotherapeutic treatments. Medical specialties have been established to provide the precise knowledge and training a physician needs to treat specific disorders with maximum competence. Therefore, if your student is diagnosed with a psychiatric disorder, it is in his or her best interest to be evaluated and followed by a psychiatrist for medication (and to receive psychotherapy from a well-trained mental health professional).

Finally, when parents suspect that their child is troubled but are unsure about how serious the situation is or about how to discuss it with their child, they should always feel free to consult professionals at the counseling center for assistance and guidance. Parents can also consult online resources, such as the Jed Foundation (http://www.jedfoundation.org), for additional information and resources regarding mental health issues and the college student.[29]

In this chapter we have identified specific psychological disorders and addictive behaviors that may affect college students. These disorders include depression, anxiety, eating disorders, bipolar disorder, self-injury, schizophrenia, and substance abuse. We have delineated symptoms of each disorder and described some common treatment modalities. In addition, we have discussed alcohol and other drug abuse on the campus and offered guidelines as to how parents may intervene and access appropriate care for their student. We highlighted the importance for students experiencing psychological distress to be seen by qualified mental health care providers, and, when medication is necessary, by a psychiatrist for evaluation, treatment, and follow-up.

In the next chapter we will describe services available to students and parents on campus and highlight resources parents should be particularly aware of. Although it is disheartening to learn about the number of psychological and substance abuse problems that take place on the campus, parents may be assured that help is also available for their student.

Chapter Six

Campus Services and Resources

In the previous three chapters, we have discussed many of the challenges that college students may face on the campus. We have explored a wide range of issues and concerns, from the to-be-expected challenges inherent in the transition to college, to the more serious issues regarding untoward incidents on the campus, as well as psychological impairment and substance abuse. In this chapter, we will acquaint parents with some of the student services and resources available on the campus that can assist students in meeting the full range of challenges that they might encounter. In addition, these services and resources provide assistance to all students with regard to maintaining physical, emotional, intellectual, and spiritual wellness on the campus.

THE COUNSELING CENTER/COUNSELING AND PSYCHOLOGICAL SERVICES (CAPS)

The counseling center/CAPS offers a wide variety of counseling and psychoeducational services to the campus community. Services provided may include individual, couples, and group psychotherapy; crisis intervention; advocacy for students; consultation; psychoeducational workshops; and training about wellness and mental health issues. The professional staff is trained to provide multiculturally competent counseling to a diverse student population. The staff is usually comprised of psychologists, mental health counselors, and/or social workers, across a number of different orientation approaches. There may also be a psychiatrist or a psychiatric nurse practitioner on staff to prescribe and manage medication. If mental health care providers are not available to prescribe and monitor medication within the center, referrals to off-campus providers are most often available.

The counseling process is designed to help individuals discuss and manage concerns that interfere with their ability to succeed academically and make the most of their college experience. Some of the concerns that students discuss in counseling include

- adjustment to college life
- concentration and other academic challenges
- roommate conflicts
- social anxiety or isolation
- stress management
- substance abuse
- depression
- anxiety disorders
- relationship issues, including domestic violence
- family problems
- eating disorders
- cultural/racial concerns
- concerns about sexual orientation and/or gender identity
- anger management
- bullying and cyberbullying
- self-injurious behavior
- sexual assault

Full-time college or university students are generally eligible to use the counseling services on campus. There is usually no charge (or a minimal charge) for the services provided. In recent years, some universities have initiated a sliding scale fee schedule or have linked services to the student's health insurance as a way of covering costs. There is usually not a large out-of-pocket cost for services.

Students can generally call or e-mail the counseling center/CAPS to schedule an appointment. They should inquire as to whether or not there is a waitlist, and if so, how long will it take to be seen. If the student needs to be seen urgently, this should be clearly stated during the initial contact. Some counseling centers/CAPS will provide "triage" to determine whether a student must be seen immediately.

For the most part, everything that students share with a mental health care provider is held in strict confidence. No information is released to college staff, to parents, or to outside agencies without the students' written consent, unless they are a danger to themselves or to others, involved in child or elder abuse, or by court order. It should also be noted that a student's file or record at the counseling center/CAPS is entirely separate from his or her academic record and cannot be released without written authorization.

Due to the large increase in the number of students seeking counseling services on campus, some universities have instituted a limit to the number of sessions students can have each academic year (generally between six and twelve sessions). However, most universities have a referral list of outside professionals who can provide counseling and psychotherapy to students in an off-campus setting, if needed. These providers usually charge customary fees; however, they may have a reduced, sliding scale rate for students, and they may also accept insurance reimbursement.

The counseling center/CAPS may also provide group counseling and psychotherapy, which allows students to share common concerns, get support and feedback, and find solutions to a variety of problems. Mental health providers typically meet with student groups on a weekly basis about such issues as stress management, body image, eating disorders, developing social skills, developing coping skills, interpersonal relating, the transition to college, and coping with grief and loss. Students can call the counseling center/CAPS or visit the website to see what types of groups are offered.

The counseling center/CAPS also provides psychoeducational programs and activities to help raise student awareness about mental health issues, as well as programs to promote emotional and physical wellness. Some examples of common outreach services include workshops on stress reduction, eating disorders, relationship abuse, social anxiety, multicultural issues, and anger management, as well as screening for depression, anxiety, and other mental health concerns.

Parents often wonder how to approach the topic of counseling with their sons or daughters, who may, understandably, resist the idea and argue that they have their parents or friends to turn to. Some positive aspects of counseling that parents can highlight with their son or daughter are as follows:

- The counseling relationship is completely confidential. This differs from relationships with family or friends, where the student can only hope that his or her privacy will be respected. Counselors, however, are bound by confidentiality laws and by ethical standards. Unless someone is in immediate danger to harm themselves or others, all conversations with counselors are private and confidential.
- The therapeutic relationship is not reciprocal. This means that the focus of therapy is on the client, not on the counselor, who is there to listen empathically and devote all of his or her attention to the client's concerns. Some clients find that simply being listened to without interruption is therapeutic in and of itself.
- The counselor has completed years of professional training and has learned a variety of methods and approaches to resolving problems and fostering insight. Therefore, the counselor has the skills to effectively help the client change in ways that are healthy and productive.

- A client can depend on the counselor to meet with him or her consistently at an appointed time.
- In times of crisis, the counselor can advocate on behalf of the client with faculty regarding such issues as extensions on assignments and excused absences. The counselor can also advocate on behalf of the client with other campus personnel for special needs accommodations and other considerations.

Parents who believe that counseling is necessary but find it difficult to approach their child about this topic should feel free to call their college or university counseling center/CAPS for additional suggestions about how to motivate their child to seek counseling. Parents should also call the counseling center/CAPS if they believe that their child is in danger of harming himself or herself or others. If parents are concerned that the danger is acute, they are advised to contact campus security or the local police department to access immediate help.

As a parent you should be aware that once your child has entered counseling, a mental health provider cannot give you feedback about your child's attendance or progress without a signed authorization for release of information. Certainly, as a parent you should feel free to ask your child about whether he or she has followed through and is attending sessions, while appreciating that there are some issues that your child may wish to keep private.

Parents can learn about the full range of services offered by the counseling center/CAPS and about the professional staff by consulting their website.[1]

OFFICE OF STUDENT RETENTION/STUDENT SUCCESS

Many campuses have an office of student retention/student success that offers guidance, troubleshooting, and assistance with navigating the campus environment. The goal of this office is to facilitate the retention and persistence of students through the completion of their degree. This office may be involved in creating and implementing new student (and new parent) orientation programs, as well as advocate for and implement first-year seminars or other structured first-year experiences.

Some offices track the midsemester grades and class attendance of entering students, reaching out to those who appear to be struggling. These offices may also advocate on behalf of students for such issues as class changes, excused absences, incompletes, extensions on assignments, and accommodations.

All student retention/student success staff are well informed about the other student services available on the campus and make appropriate referrals as needed. They also offer tips for academic success on their respective websites, in workshops, and in other presentations.

If you are concerned that your son or daughter is missing classes or struggling academically, please encourage him or her to contact this office. If there is a family crisis that necessitates your student missing class or that is creating distractions for your student, let the office of student retention/student success know and request that the office notify faculty about absences and missed assignments. Without disclosing personal details, this office can advocate for your student at his or her request.[2]

HEALTH SERVICES

The university health service provides accessible and quality health care to all students. It also provides wellness programs and educational information so that students can learn to identify health concerns and the need for appropriate and timely medical treatment.

The university health service understands that college students are often under a great deal of academics, financial, and social stress. The health services works to help the student cope with these issues in a physically healthy way. On many campuses, health services works in partnership with the psychological counseling and the drug and alcohol programs offered at the university. In fact, on some campuses, these services are integrated and can be found in a wellness center or student health center.

The student health service provides health care to students including evaluation and treatment of illnesses and injuries, women's health care, immunizations, and treatment of prevention of STDs. Students should be encouraged to fill out health forms completely and accurately (this information is not part of the student's academic record). By thoroughly and candidly reporting their medical history, students give health care professionals the opportunity to provide the best care possible. Students with significant health concerns (for example, diabetes, seizure disorders, hemophilia) should make health services aware of their health concerns at the start of the academic year. Students should also advise health services of such medical situations as autoimmune illnesses or pregnancy, which might alter how a health care provider would intervene medically. Parents can certainly consult with health services about concerns they have about their son or daughter, while recognizing that health care providers cannot share specific identifiable information without a written authorization for release of information by the student.[3]

ALCOHOL AND OTHER DRUG SERVICES

Many colleges and universities offer alcohol and substance abuse prevention, education, and support services to help reduce the instances of abuse of alcohol and other drugs and its many negative consequences, which can be medical, academic, interpersonal, and even legal. Most services provide education, outreach, and intervention.

This service provides a wide range of educational programming to students, staff, administrators, faculty, and often to parents. Educational programming for students and parents may begin during new student orientation, in which the campus alcohol and other drug policy may be introduced and statistics regarding alcohol and other drug use and its consequences on the campus may be offered, as well as suggestions for how students can be involved in organizations dedicated to harm reduction.

Staff members also collaborate with other student services and with student organizations to design and implement educational programs. Examples include the link between alcohol/drug use and sexual assault, the abuse of prescription medications, and recommendations for safe spring breaks. This office also offers alcohol-free social programs and events. It may also invite outside speakers to present intensive programs to all campus constituencies, such as those provided by the BACCHUS Network (www.bacchusnetwork.org).

One way that students can become involved with alcohol and other drug prevention is by becoming peer alcohol educators, who meet with students one-on-one, make classroom presentations, and design their own programs regarding alcohol and other drug abuse. The staff of alcohol and other drug services extensively trains peer alcohol educators to ensure that they are conveying accurate information to students.

Alcohol and other drug services also offer alcohol and other drug screenings and provide referral information for off-campus substance abuse treatment and detoxification facilities, as well as for local twelve-step groups. In some instances alcohol and other drug services also provide assessment and evidenced-based intervention for students who are abusing substances and/or for students who have violated the alcohol and other drugs policy on their campus. At a minimum, this office will direct students to online educational resources and courses regarding abuse of alcohol and other drugs.

Parents can learn about the full range of services provided by this office by visiting their website. In addition, if you as a parent are concerned about your own son's or daughter's abuse of alcohol or other substances, you should feel free to consult with alcohol and other drug services about how to access evaluation and intervention for your child.[4]

OFFICE OF RESIDENTIAL LIFE

The primary purpose of the office of residential life is to provide a safe, secure, and inclusive environment in which the intellectual, interpersonal, psychological, and cultural development of each resident is facilitated. The professional and paraprofessional staff of the office of residential life is dedicated to creating a strong sense of community, and in turn, there is a high expectation of responsibility and respect placed upon residents.

Each resident is assigned a resident assistant, who has been extensively trained to be a campus resource, available to answer questions about campus life and living in community. Resident assistants have the responsibility to maintain order and compliance with the code of conduct in the residence hall, and they may be called upon to help residents negotiate roommate conflicts. They may also be on call after hours in order to respond to any incidents that may arise. Resident assistants provide educational programming for residents on such topics as alcohol and other drug awareness, living in community, diversity, negotiating roommate conflict, sexual assault, and other issues relevant to campus life.

Resident assistants make themselves available to assist their residents with the transition to college and other concerns. Frequently, they are on the frontline of identifying residents who may be experiencing problems, and they often make referrals to other student services, such as the counseling center/CAPS. Resident assistants are supervised by residence hall directors or area coordinators, who typically hold a master's degree in counseling, higher education administration, or college student administration.[5]

If parents become concerned about their student's living situation (for example, a roommate conflict, an unsatisfactory room assignment, or need for an accommodation), they should ask their child to *first* attempt to resolve the issue on his or her own with the residential life staff. If their child has been unsuccessful, parents can advocate on his or her behalf.

OFFICE OF DISABILITIES/LEARNING NEEDS

The office of disabilities/learning needs assists students diagnosed with a disability (learning or physical) to participate equally and fully in academic and social activities. The service offers documentation and/or determination of a disability. The office of disabilities/learning needs also provides individual assessment of strengths and challenges and the development of an accommodation plan to help the student. Some disabilities/learning needs offices provide intensive one-on-one tutoring, mentoring, and counseling, as well as workshops on such topics as time management, effective note-taking, improving concentration, and study skills.

Office of disabilities/learning needs also collaborates with faculty, administrators, and university staff and advocates to ensure that students receive reasonable and appropriate accommodations for diagnosed disabilities. According to Section 504 of the Federal Rehabilitation Act of 1973 and Title III of the Americans with Disabilities Act of 1990, anyone diagnosed with a disability should be offered reasonable and appropriate auxiliary aids and services to assist otherwise qualified persons in achieving access to its programs, services, and facilities.[6]

The Americans with Disabilities Act Amended Act (ADAA) of 2008 has widened the rights of students to accommodations and extended the definition of disability. Parents interested in learning more about their college student's right to accommodations should consult www.eeoc.gov/laws/statutes/adaa_info.cfm. Examples of reasonable accommodations include extended time for tests, note-taking, sign-language interpreters, taped textbooks, and private rooms for test taking.[7]

Parents should be aware that a student diagnosed with a psychiatric disorder may qualify for disability services and should consider registering with the disabilities/learning needs office in order to benefit from special accommodations. Parents of previously diagnosed students or of students who are struggling academically are encouraged to explore disability services on their child's campus.

OFFICE OF MULTICULTURAL AFFAIRS

The office of multicultural affairs (OMA) works to promote an inclusive campus learning environment for all students of the college community. The OMA collaborates with other university departments to develop educational and experiential programs and initiatives that are infused into all aspects of student life and across the curriculum.

The OMA works to support the continued development of the multicultural *awareness* of the self within a cultural context, *knowledge* of cultures that vary from one's own, and the *skills* necessary to communicate effectively across cultures, by providing training in these areas to college students, administrators, and faculty. The OMA also seeks to promote open and ongoing dialogue among students of diverse backgrounds, traditions, and worldviews.

OMA supports the recruitment and retention of historically underrepresented students. These students are often underrepresented by ethnicity, socioeconomic status, race, gender, religion, or sexual identity. The OMA not only provides support for these students, but also provides campus outreach so that the entire university community can join in promoting a welcoming learning environment for all students.

On some campuses, the OMA staff serves as mentors and advisors to student groups and organizations related to a diverse student population. Examples include the Black Student Alliance, Muslim Student Association, African-Caribbean Student Association, Hispanic/Latino Heritage, American Indian Student Union, Asian/Pacific Islander Student Association, Gay/Lesbian/Bi-sexual/Transgender Alliance, and the International Student Organization. The OMA may also oversee the commemoration of annual diversity-related programs such as Black History Month, Coming Out Week, AIDS Awareness Week, or Latino(a) Heritage Week. This office may also conduct periodic assessments of campus climate in order to ensure that it is hospitable for all constituencies. The OMA may additionally provide leadership training for underserved student populations.[8]

Parents are encouraged to view the OMA as a potential resource for all students. Attending a variety of cross-cultural events, joining cultural organizations, and participating in creating a diversity-positive campus benefits the entire college student population.

CAMPUS MINISTRIES

Some universities have a religious affiliation, and while others do not, they may nevertheless provide support for various religious groups on campus. Students of faith who wish to explore their spirituality may seek out the campus ministries office to obtain information about the services they provide to support personal and spiritual growth.

In general, campus ministries provide prayer services, observances of holy days, and celebrations of rituals within various faith traditions, in addition to retreats that allow students to reflect upon their spiritual development, their core values and beliefs, and their faith formation. Campus ministries may also encourage the development of programs and activities across faith traditions to expose students to religious diversity. Examples may include interfaith Passover seders, Christmas/Hanukkah/Kwanza celebrations, and Ramadan observances.[9]

Although completely separate offices, the counseling center and campus ministries may work together to assist students having emotional difficulties. When in crisis, some religious students may feel more comfortable initially reaching out to a campus ministries professional than to a counseling staff member. Parents should keep this potential resource in mind if their child is struggling and in need of guidance. They should also be assured that campus ministries staff will refer students to the counseling center when that is the most appropriate course of action.

In addition, many campus ministries offices and organizations provide outreach, service learning, and a variety of volunteer opportunities to serve marginalized populations, to give back to the surrounding community, and to promote social justice. Parents should be aware that engaging in volunteer activities is also a good way for their students to meet like-minded peers in a constructive context.

INTERNATIONAL STUDIES OFFICE

The purpose of the international studies office is to provide service and support to the college's or university's international students, scholars, and researchers. The international studies office also contributes to intellectual and cultural diversity on the campus through its service to the international student community.

To accomplish its mission, the international studies office generates required legal documents for nonimmigrant students; provides advisory and counseling services; and serves as a liaison to university departments, U.S. and foreign government agencies, and the greater community. In addition, this office works to facilitate the assimilation of international students into the larger college community and contributes to the international community's cross-cultural appreciation and understanding. In many cases it also provides English language training to individuals seeking to improve their English language skills to prepare for admission to U.S. universities or colleges whose primary instructional language is English.[10]

ACADEMIC RESOURCE SERVICES

The academic resource center works to provide students with a wide array of support services to enable them to become independent self-learners. It offers all students the opportunity to receive one-on-one tutoring and, in some cases, provides ongoing coaching in writing and math skills. Some academic resource centers also provide workshops on such topics as study skills, time management, test preparation, and reducing academic stress. Generally, academic resources centers are user friendly, in that appointments are not required for regular services and students may walk in any time during office hours. In some cases, academic resource centers work with the office of disabilities/learning needs to provide accommodations such as test-taking in a private setting, note-taking services, and books on tape for students with disabilities.[11]

Parents are advised to refer their college students to this excellent resource as soon as they begin to express concerns about their academic functioning.

CAREER SERVICES

Career services provides students with the tools they need to explore and select an academic major, learn about careers, identify their own career interests, and secure an internship and ultimately a position post-graduation. Many career services currently offer a wealth of Web-based resources and services that provide students with access to job postings, the ability to upload their resumés and send them to potential employers, receive infomation about upcoming events, complete online career interest inventories, engage in a resumé review, and participate in other services.

Because this office provides assistance through all four years of college and sometimes beyond to alumni, students should register and set up an account with the Web-based resources available through career services upon their arrival on campus. During freshman year students can immediately begin to explore their interests and strengths as they consider possible majors. In subsequent years, they can use Web-based resources to secure an internship, explore careers, and receive assistance with their job search.

Students can (and should) also meet with career counselors face-to-face to receive career counseling, to engage in mock interviews, to flesh out the results of interest and/or personality inventories they have taken, and to address special needs or concerns they might have regarding securing an internship or a position.[12]

At a minimum, parents should encourage their student to visit the career services website, which often contains a wealth of information delineated for each year of college, and to attend workshops that are offered on every aspect of the career development process.

OFFICE OF STUDENT AFFAIRS/STUDENT LIFE

The office of student affairs/student life often serves as a gateway to, and provides supervision of, many of the student services delineated above. This office may also include associate student affairs deans who oversee fraternities and sororities, student activities, student media, cultural and entertainment events, the student union, student government, leadership development and training, and most student clubs and organizations. Students can become acquainted with the full range of cocurricular options available to them by visiting the office of student affairs/student life website and by consulting their student handbook.[13]

Some student affairs/student life offices include a liaison for parents, and they may produce a parents handbook that provides a wealth of information about campus life. Parents and students should be aware that this office is critical for the facilitation of student involvement and engagement, which in turn promotes student retention and persistance through graduation. Parents whose college student is feeling isolated and/or complaining that "there is nothing to do on campus" should direct him or her to visit this office, or at the very least to explore the website to learn about the abundance of opportunities available for involvement on campus.[14]

STUDENT FINANCIAL SERVICES

Student financial services (SFS) assists parents and students with making higher education affordable by informing them about the application and documentation process that needs to be completed in order to access financial aid. Most SFS offices maintain websites with a wealth of information, including types of financial aid, how to apply, online forms, and information about on-campus employment/workstudy.

Types of financial aid include federal based, state based, institutional based, and a wealth of outside scholarships. An example of these scholarships is the Teacher Education Assistance for College and Higher Education (TEACH) Grant, which offers up to $4,000 per year for students majoring in education who will teach underserved populations. SFS websites also offer parents and students links to other sources of scholarship information such as the College Board (http://www.collegeboard.org) or College Connection (http://www.collegescholarships.com). Some SFS websites also provide links to financial literacy and debt management tutorials for parents and students, as well as links to resources for veterans and other specific cohorts.

Many SFS websites include special sections for parents with information such as how to directly access an SFS staff member, and they remind parents to talk to their student about signing a release of information form, as students' financial information is protected under the Family Educational Rights and Privacy Act (FERPA). It also includes advice to parents about such matters as the range of payment plans, meal plans, and tuition insurance programs.

SFS is staffed by financial aid counselors who will provide accurate information to students and parents. They are generally available for face-to-face meetings, and parents should not hesitate to call an SFS counselor with any financial aid inquiry.[15]

CAMPUS SAFETY AND SECURITY

Students often view this office as one that imposes parking fines, tows their vehicles, and metes out other sanctions. However, parents and students should be aware that the primary pupose of this office is to provide a safe living and learning environment to all members of the campus community.

Students who have concerns about their safety—for example, if they are being stalked, threatened, or find themselves in a domestic violence situation—can turn to the campus safety and security office for guidance and information about safety measures. Certainly, students who have been the victims of crime, such as rape, burglary, break-ins, or cyberbullying, can turn to campus safety and security for assistance.

In times of crisis, such as acts of terrorism, the presence of violent persons on the campus, hostage situations, or national disasters, campus safety and security takes the lead in resolving these situations and in coordinating the campus response. Often, this office has an emergency notification system that informs the campus community about crisis situations. Generally, students must register their cell phone numbers in order to receive notifications.

Campus safety and security also creates programs and publications with safety tips for students, making them aware of their own role in safeguarding their possessions and living space. They may also provide an escort service, as well as emergency phones throughout the campus to access help quickly. In addtion, this office compiles crime statistics for the instituion, as required by the Cleary Act. Generally, parents and students can access this report on the campus safety and security website.[16]

Parents who have concerns about their student's safety should feel free to consult with this office and to encourage their son or daughter to receive guidance from this campus resource as well.

OFFICE OF THE OMBUDSPERSON

Many colleges and universities provide the services of a designated ombudsperson to all campus constituencies, including students. The ombudsperson is a neutral, independent, and confidential resource whom students can turn to for problems related to harassment, discrimination, or the unfair application of a campus policy. Students can bring their concern, grievance, or complaint to the ombudsperson, who will listen objectively, suggest remedial steps, and attempt to mediate disputes whenever possible.

The ombudsperson will provide students with specific policies and procedures that are relevant to their complaint or concern. For example, if a student believes that he or she has been sexually harassed, the ombudsperson will give the student the institution's sexual harassment policy document and review all courses of action available, internally and externally, including legal options. The ombudsperson does not adjudicate grievances, but he or she can supply information, recommend solutions, and provide guidance to the student.[17]

As a parent, you should know that the ombudsperson is a confidential source of assistance for your student, who is especially useful in instances of potential harassment or discrimination.

HOW PARENTS CAN LEARN MORE ABOUT STUDENT SERVICES

Parents can learn more about services on campus by participating in orientation activities and other events designated for parents. Attending orientation events and speaking with college and university staff and faculty will give parents a sense of their student's new environment, and in-depth information about the resources available. Attending orientation events will also demonstrate to your student that you are interested in and concerned about his or her college experience.

In addition, every college and university has a website that is filled with information about both academic and campus life. Most colleges and universities are structurally divided into an academic division and a student affairs division. We encourage parents to pay particular attention to the student services and campus life categories of the student affairs web page. There, you will find extensive information about the campus counseling center/ CAPS and other services, including and in addition to those described above (for example, off-campus housing, student legal services, commuter services, women's center, study abroad, recreation and intramurals). Many of the student service websites offer a variety of online resources; some offer helpful guidelines specifically geared toward parents. In addition, parents should never hesitate to call a student service office directly for more information. Parents should be reassured that regardless of the concern or challenge their student might encounter, there are professional services available on the campus that offer substantial assistance.

In this chapter, we have introduced parents to a number of student services and campus resources available to their students for troubleshooting problems, for personal and career counseling, for the enhancement of academic success, for engagement in cocurricular activities, and for accommodations and mentoring. These services and resources are there to promote the overall wellness and success of college students across several dimensions: academic, physical, emotional, spiritual, interpersonal, financial, and professional. In the next chapter, we will explore specific strategies and approaches that we believe are effective for promoting and maintaining wellness and academic success on the campus.

Chapter Seven

Promoting Emotional Wellness and Student Success

Some Approaches That Work

In the previous chapter, we discussed some of the student services and campus resources available to assist students when a problem arises, which also facilitate their emotional, intellectual, spiritual, physical, and vocational development. In this chapter, we will explore some of the specific approaches, strategies, and factors that significantly contribute to student success and wellness. We will offer suggestions for effective parent–college student communication and discuss strategies for stress reduction and the development of coping skills, positive self-talk, recognition of signature strengths, and enhancing self-esteem. Finally, we will delineate key factors that have been found to be critical to promoting student success and wellness.

EFFECTIVE PARENT–COLLEGE STUDENT COMMUNICATION

Perhaps the most important thing a parent can do to help their child succeed in college is to develop and maintain healthy and respectful communication patterns. For some parents this may mean building on an already positive relationship and only making slight adjustments. For others it will mean developing a new way of relating with your student. Nevertheless, regardless of where your relationship falls on this continuum, the start of college is an excellent time to reflect on how well you communicate with your emerging adult and to make appropriate changes as needed.

First and foremost is acknowledging your student's newfound independence and emerging adult role and validating their individuality. Parents should work toward developing adult-to-adult communication, characterized by mutual respect and give-and-take. Many parents assume they know exactly what their child is thinking, feeling, or doing in response to certain situations. At one time in his or her life this may have been true. However, as individuals grow, change, and are exposed to new people, ideas, points of view, and cultures, their perspectives also grow and change. It is more helpful, therefore, to acknowledge this change by asking your child questions about how he or she feels or what he or she wishes to do rather than to assume that you know the answer.

The goal of communication with your emerging adult is to build a strong sense of connection and empathy, rather than to perpetuate the voice of authority—that is, telling your child what to do. When your student was a child these patterns of communication were most likely helpful. You were able to solve many of your child's problems by simply telling your child what her or his course of action should be. However, this pattern of communication does not provide an opportunity for problem solving or for starting the process of managing one's own life. Further, authoritarian or controlling patterns of communication often interfere with developing and maintaining a healthy, mutually respectful relationship, rather than promoting it.

Parents, therefore, may of course offer their opinion while giving equal weight to that of their child. It is wise for parents to avoid using statements such as you "must" or "should," which can be perceived as directives and shut down communication. It is suggested that even before offering their own opinion or advice, parents develop the habit of first asking what the student believes would be a good course of action.

Let your student know that you expect to have disagreements with him or her, and that's OK. Disagreement is not the end of the world, nor of the relationship. At times, resolving disagreements will be possible by using good listening and respectful communication skills. However, at times you and your student may have to agree to disagree, and leave it at that. When disagreements become heated and tempers begin to flare, it is advisable to take a time-out and return to the discussion after all parties have had an opportunity to calm down.[1]

Many students worry about burdening their parents with their problems. Parents should, therefore, let their student know that they are interested and want to know about his or her experiences, both good and bad. Directly let students hear that you want to know if they are having a difficult time, and that you want to be there for them. Even if they choose not to reach out to you, giving them permission leaves a pathway open and provides relief. For example, you might say, "I understand that things may not always go so well, so if you are stressed out or worried about something, please know I'm interested and you can speak to me."

Negotiate with your son or daughter about the frequency of contact you will have with him or her. Ask your student how often he or she would like to have contact with you, while also expressing what level of contact is comfortable for you. Coming to a mutual decision about communication lets your child know that you are interested in maintaining contact, while also respecting his or her privacy and growing self-reliance and autonomy.

Again, we want to acknowledge cultural differences in communication patterns between parents and grown children. In some cultures, it is the norm for parents to maintain an authoritative role and set the ground rules for communication. Nevertheless, we encourage *all* parents to consider altering their pattern of communication with their college student in ways that acknowledge his or her growing maturity and foster the student's ability to solve problems and make decisions.

Much has been written about active and reflective listening as a way of improving parent-child communication. As the parent of a college student, learning some of these skills can clearly help enhance your communication and, as a result, enhance your overall relationship with your student.[2] Some key concepts include the following:

- Listen more than speak. Listen closely and really concentrate on what your child is saying, rather than focusing on what you want to say next. Take the stance of respectful listening to your child's point of view.
- Try to avoid distractions or multitasking while your son or daughter is speaking. Give him or her your undivided attention.
- Do not respond immediately. Take a breath and gather your thoughts before you speak, especially if you are tempted to disagree or to be critical.
- Avoid finishing your student's thoughts and sentences. Often what you say may not be accurate, and for sure, it will shut down communication.
- Avoid using questions that elicit yes or no answers. These types of questions stop the flow of conversation. Instead, ask open-ended questions and make action-oriented statements. For example, instead of asking "Is everything OK?" you might say, "Tell me about how things are going for you."
- Reflect back to your student what you have just heard him or her say, to make sure that you have heard accurately. For example, you might say, "Let me make sure that I understand what you're saying. You're telling me that . . ." This will not only show your child that you are interested in what she or he is saying, it will also help avoid miscommunication.
- Don't forget to give praise and make loving statements to your student, as he or she will never tire of that. Don't hesitate to say, "I'm so proud of you . . . Great job! . . . You're the best . . . I feel lucky to be your dad . . . You're such a good person. . . ."

REDUCING STRESS AND DEVELOPING COPING SKILLS

Stress is a psychological and physical response to changes and the demands of life. It is a personal experience, in that what is extremely stressful for one individual may not be stressful to another at all. Both positive and negative life changes can lead to the experience of stress. For example, one student may feel joy and a sense of accomplishment about graduating from college, while another may primarily experience anxiety about the future. Working part-time may be seen as a break from academic endeavors, or as a drain of time and energy. Most often, people report a stress response when their coping skills have been overwhelmed.

Stressors can come from internal or external sources. For example, things like academic demands, overcrowding in a classroom, relationship conflict, and work pressures would be considered external stressors. Things like poor diet, too little exercise, and negative and self-defeating thinking would be considered internal. You can help your student identify particular external and internal sources of stress as a way to begin the process of stress reduction.

The way a person handles stress can either improve the situation or create more stress. For example, when coping skills are lacking or overwhelmed, some individuals may turn to alcohol or drugs in an attempt to manage their stress. This strategy may help mitigate stress in the short run; however, in the long run it can create a new set of problems related to substance abuse or dependency. A student who uses avoidance and procrastination as a way of alleviating the pressures of school may feel some momentary relief; however, as time progresses, he or she will only become more anxious and overwhelmed as schoolwork begins to pile up to levels that are far more difficult to manage.

Sometimes there is nothing that can be done to prevent a stressor from occurring; however, the experience of stress can be reduced or eliminated with practice and improved coping skills. You can help reduce your student's level of stress by encouraging him or her to develop the following coping strategies:

- Recognize signs of stress and intervene early on, rather than allowing it to spiral out of control.
- Exercise regularly, including both aerobic activities (which have been shown to decrease stress and improve mood) and calming activities, such as yoga and tai chi, which promote mindfulness and being in the moment.
- Practice assertive behaviors and responses to overcome feelings of powerlessness and helplessness. For example, saying no and meaning it can reduce stress immeasurably. Believe that it's OK to set limits with others in order to take care of yourself.

- Increase social contact and support, for comfort, empathy, and companionship.
- Learn effective time-management skills in order to live a balanced life. Make time for studying, socializing, exercising, and having fun.
- Engage in enjoyable activities and take time for relaxation every day. Recharging one's batteries is a must for coping effectively. No one copes when running on empty.
- Let go of perfectionism and set reasonable, attainable expectations for all areas of life. Insisting on being perfect at everything is a setup for frustration.
- Practice relaxation techniques such as progressive muscle relaxation, deep breathing, and visual imagery on a regular basis.[3]
- Accept stress as a normal part of being alive. Try not to catastrophize about being stressed out.
- For each of the recommendations above, make use of campus facilities and resources, for example the fitness center, counseling center, and wellness center. Check out the Student Activities website for classes in yoga, tai chi, karate, Pilates, dance, relaxation techniques, and other wellness and stress reduction strategies. The campus is filled with experts on academic success strategies, emotional wellness, health, fitness, time management, career coaching, and many other areas. Use them!

MAINTAINING PERSPECTIVE: CHANGING THOUGHTS AND SELF-TALK

Helping your student to identify problematic thinking patterns will help him or her to change these patterns, reduce stress, maintain focus, and increase a sense of well-being. For all of us, problematic thinking patterns can interfere with the quality of our lives; negativity, self-reproach, and unnecessary worry are examples of the type of thoughts that can make life difficult. Understanding common cognitive distortions—that is, inaccurate, self-defeating, perfectionistic thinking patterns—can help students recognize and change their own unhelpful self-talk. This approach to improving mood and reducing anxiety comes from a psychotherapy approach called cognitive behavioral therapy (CBT). Most college and university counseling centers offer CBT as an effective and relatively short-term approach to resolving emotional problems and maintaining a healthy perspective.

CBT techniques are also an excellent self-help strategy for students. For example, in his book *Feeling Good: The New Mood Therapy*, Dr. David D. Burns outlines common distortions in thinking to which we are all prone.[4] However, depressed and anxious individuals may engage in many more of these distortions than nondepressed persons. Some common distortions are:

- Catastrophizing, which means blowing negative events out of proportion and losing all sense of perspective. For example, a college student may view one poor grade on a test as a sign that he or she will likely fail out of school.
- Jumping to conclusions, especially negative conclusions without sufficient evidence. For example, if a peer walks by your student without acknowledging him or her, your child may jump to the conclusion that the peer actively dislikes him or her (as opposed to simply being lost in thought).
- "Should" statements, in which we attempt to motivate ourselves with "should," "must," and "need to" absolutes (for example, "I should be able to excel at everything I do"). They usually do not work and only foster a sense of guilt, frustration, and failure. Sometimes we apply these statements to others, which is usually a recipe for resentment, anger, and disappointment (for example, "My roommate should have invited me to that concert and should have known how bad it would make me feel to be excluded").
- Personalization takes place when we believe that we are responsible for negative outcomes and behavior by others, when we are not. For example, your student's roommate is in a bad mood and your student blames himself or herself for causing it.
- All-or-nothing thinking, in which we see things in absolute categories, perceived as good or bad, right or wrong, black or white. For example, if your child's performance is less than perfect, he or she considers himself or herself a failure.
- Over-generalizing, which entails seeing one negative event as a never-ending pattern of failure or negativity. For example, a student might experience one minor hassle over the course of a day and conclude that the entire day was awful. More seriously, a student may have one aspect of life not go well (for example, not dating) and conclude that his or her entire life is terrible or not worth it.
- Disqualifying the positive, in which we focus on negative experiences while ignoring our positive experiences and accomplishments. For example, a student may receive one "B" grade at the end of a semester and disregard an otherwise stellar academic record, as well as other achievements such as volunteering and establishing good friendships.
- Emotional reasoning, in which we interpret what we are feeling as a fact. We believe that our emotions define reality. For example a student might say, "I feel like a loser; therefore I must be one."[5]

By understanding and recognizing these distortions (in themselves and in their children) parents can become better listeners and helpers. For example, if your child calls and is in a bad mood, you might assume that their emotional state is directly related to you or something that you've done or said. This reaction, however, may be a cognitive distortion (jumping to conclusions and personalization). It very well could be that your child is just having a bad day for some other reason, and his or her tone and mood have nothing to do with you. Therefore, instead of getting angry or defensive, you might be able to take a step back and just listen or simply acknowledge what your child is feeling. In addition, by recognizing these distortions, you will be able to help your child see them, as well. For example, if your child is worried and afraid of failing out of school after one bad exam grade, you can help your child put this in perspective by pointing out that this is simply one piece of data about his or her performance.

If you believe that your student can benefit from learning more about cognitive behavioral therapy (CBT), refer him or her to the on-campus counseling center, which is likely to offer this approach.

CULTIVATING HAPPINESS AND RECOGNIZING SIGNATURE STRENGTHS

Based on the work of Martin Seligman at the University of Pennsylvania, positive psychology is a relatively new branch of psychology that seeks to help individuals identify "signature strengths" that enable them to thrive. Examples of signature strengths are the capacity for love and work, courage, compassion, resilience, creativity, curiosity, integrity, self-knowledge, moderation, self-control, and wisdom. Positive psychology suggests that if people can identify their signature strengths, and then incorporate these strengths into their studies and occupation, they will not only increase their level of happiness, but they will also be more successful.[6]

Positive psychology also promotes the intentional cultivation of positive emotions such as happiness, well-being, gratitude, and optimism. Extensive research investigating factors that promote happiness found that close relationships with friends and family, spirituality, altruism, counting one's blessings, savoring the moment, thanking mentors, taking care of one's body (especially by engaging in regular exercise), utilizing strategies for coping and stress reduction, and engaging in activities that tap into one's strengths are significant contributors to a sense of well-being.[7]

Some activities suggested by positive psychologists based on these research findings are the following:

- Engage in volunteer activities that clearly help others and make a difference.
- Keep a daily "gratitude journal" in which you jot down the little and big things for which you are thankful, preferably at the end of each day.
- Spend time with friends or family members each day.

- Engage in a daily "three good things" exercise in which you recall three positive events that took place during the day.
- Discover your "signature strengths" by taking the positive psychology inventory available at http://www.authentichappiness.com.
- Choose activities that maximize your signature strengths.
- Choose a career that maximizes your signature strengths.
- Seek out pleasant activities on a daily basis.

Parents should encourage their college student to use campus services and resources to help him or her engage in activities that develop those attributes that have been shown to contribute to happiness and that further enhance his or her signature strengths.

INCREASING SELF-ESTEEM AND SELF-RESPECT

In chapter 4, we discussed some of the unpleasant realities of campus life, including the availability of alcohol and other drugs, the access to sexual partners (willing and unwilling), the pressure to be thin, participating in unhealthy relationships, bullying, cyberbullying, and hazing, among others. There may also be a culture of peer pressure that condones behavior that is unhealthy and self-destructive and runs counter to achieving academic success, personal satisfaction, and happiness.

As a parent, you may well be asking yourself: Why do some students succumb to these pressures, while others do not? How can I help *my* student to withstand the external and internal pressures to engage in unhealthy behaviors? In a nutshell, the answer is that students with high self-esteem who respect themselves are less likely to engage in behaviors that harm themselves and others.

Parents can help inoculate students against toxic peer pressure by assisting them in raising their self-esteem. They can do so both directly, by the way they communicate with their student, and indirectly by encouraging him or her to engage in constructive on-campus activities and to get professional help when needed.

Some specific steps that parents can take are as follows:

- As previously noted, parents can make sure that their communication style with their student is mutually respectful, adult-to-adult, and geared toward problem solving.[8]
- Parents should not hesitate to praise accomplishments and to verbally affirm their student as a valuable person.
- Parents are asked to keep criticism to a minimum.

- Parents should let their child know directly that she or he deserves to be happy and to be treated with respect by everyone.
- If you, as a parent, believe that your child is being mistreated by a roommate, friend, or romantic partner, tell him or her about your concern.
- If you, as a parent, believe that your child is engaging in self-destructive, unhealthy behavior (such as abusing substances, self-injury, or disordered eating), get him or her professional help. Tell your child that he or she deserves to be well, and you will do everything you can to help.
- Point your child to activities that directly build self-esteem, such as volunteering and making a difference in the lives of others. Students find these activities extremely rewarding, and they do feel good about themselves by helping others. Every campus offers many volunteer activities.
- Encourage your student to get involved in peer education and advocacy groups that make a difference on campus, such as bystander intervention groups (which teach students to interrupt negative incidents such as binge drinking, sexual assault, bullying, and hate speech), alcohol peer educator groups (for example, the BACCHUS Network), or mental health educator groups (for example, Active Minds on Campus). These activities empower students to become part of the solution by helping peers.[9]
- Some campuses have student-initiated groups that directly address the topics of respect for self, peers, the campus community, diversity, the environment, and so on (for example, the Iona College Respect Campaign).[10] Encourage your student to become involved in groups like this or to promote a similar group on his or her campus.
- Support your student in exploring his or her spirituality. This does not necessarily mean greater participation in an organized religion; rather it might mean engaging in activities that explore their core values and encourage them to live their best lives.
- Engage your students in conversations about how they see themselves, what they truly want out of life, and how they envision getting there.
- Challenge any self-deprecating comments your child makes about his or her appearance, intelligence, ability, likeability, or other areas of their self-concept.
- If you see signs that your child has low self-esteem (for example, making self-deprecating comments, tolerating poor behavior from peers, being pressured into engaging in behaviors related to sex or alcohol, engaging in other unhealthy or self-sabotaging behavior), refer him or her to the counseling center. Approaches like cognitive behavioral therapy (discussed above) can directly help students address their negative self-talk and change their self-defeating behavior.

ENCOURAGING HEALTHY LIFESTYLE CHOICES

Being healthy is much more than just being disease free. It involves many dimensions and is a foundation for realizing one's potential. For students, a healthy lifestyle plays a crucial role in helping achieve personal and academic success. At college, students may have their first experience of being in charge of their own health care and wellness. It is important that students learn to take an active role in assessing their wellness and make informed choices regarding their health and health care.

Lifestyle choices play an important role in health and wellness. Healthy behaviors and choices are necessary to achieve and maintain both physical and psychological well-being. Parents ultimately cannot control the behaviors and choices of their children. However, providing information about good health and wellness practices and encouraging their student to invest time and energy in health will assist him or her in making healthier lifestyle choices.

Below are some healthy lifestyle behaviors to be encouraged in students:

- Maintain healthy body weight and eat healthfully; learn about nutrition and good eating habits. Students should be aware that with the transition to college often comes the "freshman 15," meaning that it is common for new students to put on weight during their first year of school. If this is anticipated and students understand healthy eating habits, they can plan to make healthier choices as they arrive on campus.[11]
- At the same time, students are advised not to become *overly* focused to the point of obsession regarding their weight. Rather, students are advised to set realistic expectations and maintain a healthy weight for *their* body.
- If students do become overly preoccupied with their weight and/or restrict eating, or if they engage in purging or excessive, compulsive exercising, they should seek help immediately at their student health or counseling services.
- Engage in physical activity and regular moderate exercise. This helps both physical and psychological health and reduces stress, so long as it does not become a compulsion.
- Learn and use stress reduction techniques, and take some time each day to relax and unwind. This can include things like meditation, progressive relaxation techniques, napping, listening to music, or engaging in a creative activity or some other pastime that is soothing.
- Understand safe sex practices and do not engage in unprotected sex. Regardless of their personal views or beliefs about sexual issues, students, as adults, should be aware of the risks and dangers of unprotected sex. These include unplanned, unwanted pregnancies and sexually transmitted diseases (STDs).

- Students should learn how to resist pressure and manipulation regarding sexual activities they are not comfortable with, including sexting.
- Students should get enough sleep. This is an obvious, but often overlooked, recommendation. To some extent, the stress, anxiety, and feeling of being overwhelmed that many college students report may be attributed to being physically exhausted. Many students push themselves to get by on very little sleep, without recognizing that this is *not* a healthy lifestyle choice. College students need eight hours of sleep every night in order to function academically and experience a sense of well-being.[12]
- Students should certainly seek out a medical care provider or the student health service if they are concerned about health issues.
- Students should refrain from consuming excessive quantities of alcohol or use of other substances. They should understand the risks involved, the physical and psychological dangers, and the potential for addiction.
- Students should be encouraged to get out of unhealthy relationships and be aware of the signs and symptoms of dangerous and abusive relationships. They should also understand those characteristics that constitute positive relationships and work to develop them.
- Students should be encouraged to develop realistic and attainable goals in all areas of their lives. Parents can help guide students, or they can suggest that their student contact the counseling center for help with perfectionism.
- Students should take their prescribed medications. If a student has been given medication for a psychological or physical disorder, he or she should be responsible about taking it as prescribed and following up with the health care provider. They should be made aware of possible side effects and of the risks and dangers of not complying with taking the medication, and of combining the medication with other substances (such as alcohol).
- Students do best when they develop a balanced life that includes school, friends, family, hobbies, interests, and work. Students are happier, more grounded, and better able to maintain a sense of perspective when they invest in multiple areas of their lives. For example, a student focused exclusively on his or her relationship with a romantic partner may fall apart if the relationship ends and the student has no other area of life that provides satisfaction. Alternatively, a student who focuses exclusively on academics and academic perfection may be devastated if his or her performance is less than anticipated. Developing multiple areas of one's life will help provide balance and a sense of perspective during difficult times and challenges.

Helping students understand good health practices will serve them well throughout their college years. Further, making healthy lifestyle choices now can establish wellness habits that students take with them throughout their life span.

KNOWING THE FACTORS THAT SUPPORT SUCCESS

There has been a great deal of research investigating the key factors that lead to students' performing well academically, completing a major successfully, and persisting to graduation. Findings indicate that there are factors both *inside* and *outside* of the classroom that are significant. In addition, while some of these factors are certainly related to academics, equally important are those factors that contribute to student involvement and engagement; to creating a caring, hospitable climate on the campus; and to helping students maintain emotional and physical wellness.[13]

These factors include the following:

- Your student's choice of major or of potential majors is offered on the campus.
- The course offerings within the major are interesting and varied.
- The quality of classroom instruction is excellent.
- Academic advisers are readily available and provide guidance and accurate information about course requirements and other academic issues.
- Faculty engage students outside of the classroom, for example, during office hours, by providing mentorship and review sessions, and by contributing to integrative learning processes.
- The academic climate on the campus is encouraging and anticipates student success.
- There is a first-year experience or student success course offered to all incoming students. This course is ongoing and includes classes on study skills, time management, career development, and selecting a major, as well as communication skills and recognizing the signs of psychological distress.
- There is a front-loading of social and cultural activities that assist students in feeling connected to peers and to the institution.
- There is intentional programming to make students aware of all student clubs, organizations, and activities (for example, involvement fair, club day, activities fair).
- There is intentional programming to make students aware of the student services available to them (for example, new student orientation, student services fair, websites, the student handbook, survival guide, first-year experience).[14]
- There is an academic resource office that provides tutoring on demand, and coaching in basic writing and math skills, as well as one-on-one

coaching on time management, setting and meeting academic goals, and study skills.
- There is an office of student retention or student success that coordinates the institution's multilayered retention efforts and assists students individually to persist in college.
- The institution intentionally works to create a caring, diversity-positive, hospitable community, for example during new student orientation, "welcome new student" events at the start of fall semester, "welcome transfer student" events, student-to-student mentorship programs, faculty mentor programs, and valuing diversity programs.
- The institution values and intentionally promotes a culture of courtesy, hospitality, and caring across *all* campus constituencies.
- There is an alcohol and other drugs (AOD) education/services office that educates students about the impact of AOD use and abuse on their grades, persistence to graduation, and physical health, and offers interventions on the individual, campus, and community level.
- There is a counseling center/counseling and psychological services (CAPS) that provides adequate psychological resources for the campus. including:

-
    1. A full range of mental health care providers, including a psychiatrist.
    2. Counseling and psychotherapy services for a full range of student concerns, including significant psychological impairment.
    3. No session limits or generous session allowances.
    4. No fees or low fees for services.
    5. Screening and triage to identify students best served by immediate intervention.
    6. Crisis intervention and emergency services.
    7. Ease of making appointments and timely assessment, evaluation, and referral.
    8. Educational outreach programs that provide primary prevention to many student cohorts regarding such topics as mental health issues, destigmatizing psychological treatment, alcohol and other drug use and abuse, sexual assault, relationship violence, and stress reduction.
    9. A website that provides information about services, staff appointments, and mental health issues, as well as links to other online resources for students regarding emotional wellness (for example, U.Lifeline.com, JED Foundation.org,TheTrevorProject.org, Itgetsbetter.org).[15]

Parents can enhance their student's success by encouraging him or her to make full use of the campus resources, activities, courses, and services described above. Because so much significant learning takes place outside of the classroom, parents would do well to promote involvement in clubs and activities, emphasize the concept of a *balanced* life, and destigmatize their child's using psychological or AOD services.

ADVOCATING FOR MENTAL HEALTH AND OTHER STUDENT SERVICES ON CAMPUS

Throughout this book, we have referenced an increase in the number of students coming to campus with significant mental health concerns. Further, highly publicized student suicides and on-campus shootings resulting in significant injuries and loss of lives have heightened the public's awareness about the ongoing and escalating mental health crisis in higher education.[16]

Some colleges and universities have responded by increasing funds, personnel, and resources for promoting and maintaining emotional wellness on the campus. Unfortunately, however, some of the most significant increases have taken place on campuses where tragedies have *already* occurred. It should be obvious to parents that rather than be *re*active, colleges and universities should be more *pro*active in providing adequate mental health resources *prior* to a catastrophic campus incident.

This is not meant to scare parents but to alert them to the urgency of the need for these services in order to (a) provide remedial treatment, (b) provide mandatory assessment for danger to self or others, (c) train campus constituents on recognizing the signs of possible danger to self or others, and (d) assist the institution in implementing and maintaining a campus-wide mechanism for identifying, evaluating, and intervening with students of concern who may pose a danger to self or others.

Parents can advocate for adequate mental health services by joining parent and family networks on their campus, by contacting such offices as admissions and student affairs, and by empowering their student to advocate for quality student services.

Parents and students have a right to expect the full complement of services (noted and discussed in chapter 6), and they should advocate for them. Parents are also advised to carefully consider the availability of services that support emotional, physical, spiritual, and intellectual wellness *prior* to enrollment (as discussed in chapter 2).

Today's students encounter a campus environment that is more complex, challenging, and demanding than can readily be imagined. Those campuses that provide a network of helpful resources for your child, in addition to maintaining academic excellence, are those that deserve your (and your child's) tuition dollars.

In this chapter, we discussed approaches and strategies that are supportive of maintaining student success and emotional wellness on the campus. These approaches include respectful, effective parent–college student communication and strategies for reducing stress, developing coping skills, and enhancing self-esteem. Psychological approaches that derive from cognitive behavioral therapy (CBT) and positive psychology were reviewed, and recommendations for maintaining physical health were offered. Key factors related to college success were delineated, and parents were encouraged to advocate for adequate student services and resources on the campus.

In the conclusion of this book, we will review and summarize the key points and takeaways for parents in promoting their student's success and sanity on the campus.

Conclusion

Throughout this book we have offered an insider's view of the realities of today's college campus, both positive and negative. Among the many positive aspects of college attendance and completion we have noted:

- The opportunity to complete a degree, which will, statistically, provide greater earning power across the life span and increased overall life satisfaction[1]
- The opportunity for intellectual growth and the expansion of one's worldview
- The opportunity to become exposed to a variety of disciplines and to develop significant expertise in a chosen field of study
- The opportunity to engage in the myriad student activities, clubs, organizations, and cultural events designed specifically to involve, educate, and enlighten a young adult population
- The opportunity to meet and connect with a diverse population of peers, thereby experiencing the richness of other cultures, lifestyles, values, customs, and ways of being in the world
- The opportunity to become culturally competent, which is a requisite for functioning effectively in a pluralistic global community
- The opportunity to develop autonomy, self-regulation, self-reliance, and competence
- The opportunity to learn about the world of work and to engage in internships, field experiences, on-campus employment, and other activities that foster occupational development
- The opportunity to become student leaders and peer helpers and educators
- The opportunity to be skilled decision makers and problem solvers
- The opportunity to become critical thinkers

- The opportunity to learn the value of becoming a lifelong learner
- The opportunity to participate in activities that promote civic engagement and responsible citizenship
- The opportunity to develop flexibility with regard to negotiating differences and resolving conflicts with roommates and other peers
- The opportunity to develop lifelong friendships
- The opportunity to live in community constructively and responsibly
- The opportunity to access a full range of experts and professionals whose sole purpose is to assist students in their personal, emotional, intellectual, vocational, cultural, spiritual, and interpersonal growth and development
- The opportunity to engage with faculty and other campus professionals, inside and outside of the classroom—for example, as mentors, researchers, counselors, and career consultants

We have also provided in-depth discussions of some of the potentially challenging aspects of college life that may pose difficulties for some college students. These challenges include the following:

- The presence on campus of a larger population of students with mental health problems, coupled with an increased level of severity regarding the nature of these problems
- Access to alcohol, prescription drugs, and other substances of abuse
- A reduction in external controls, monitoring, and supervision on the residential campus
- Vulnerability of college students to eating disorders, sexual assault, relationship violence, hazing, and cyberbullying
- Increased levels of stress, depression, and anxiety about personal and academic concerns, as well as about meeting the demands of adult life, reported in significant numbers within the general student population
- The ever-increasing cost of a college education, coupled with concerns about finding employment after graduation
- The uneven performance by some colleges and universities in their ability to retain students through the attainment of their undergraduate degree

To address these potentially challenging aspects of college life and to promote success and wellness, we have noted the following:

- The wealth of student services and resources available on many college and university campuses, such as career services, personal counseling, tutoring, student activities, academic advising, multicultural affairs, student retention, and alcohol and other drug services

- Psychological approaches that are effective and evidence based, such as cognitive behavioral therapy (CBT) and positive psychology, which are likely available on the campus through the counseling center/CAPS
- The importance of students developing coping skills, a sense of perspective, high self-esteem, and a healthy lifestyle, and the availability of resources on the campus to facilitate the development of these skills
- Key factors for success, such as the availability of an intensive first-year seminar/experience, excellence in classroom instruction, expectations for student success, intentional engagement of students, a diversity-positive and welcoming atmosphere, and the availability of academic advisers and mentors
- The importance of helping your student find the campus that is the best possible fit for him or her, right from the start

The main thrust of this book has been to highlight the paramount importance of the role of parents in enhancing success and emotional wellness in their college student. Specifically we have emphasized:

- The need for parents to provide both the gift of roots and the gift of wings
- The importance of parents knowing when to directly intervene and when to coach from the sidelines with regard to challenges their son or daughter may encounter
- The role of parents in helping their student select a college that is the best fit by utilizing their child's high school counselors and faculty as important resources in that process
- The likelihood that students will turn to their parents for help when they are anxious or depressed
- The importance of parents recognizing risk factors and warning signs for common psychological problems, addictions, and danger to self or others
- The need for parents to become skilled in referring their college student to appropriate student services
- The usefulness of parents being knowledgeable about key factors for the promotion of success and wellness
- The importance of parents keeping the lines of communication open with their college student, as noncritical listeners, sounding boards, and sources of comfort and support
- The importance of parents encouraging their student to maintain a healthy and balanced lifestyle
- The need for parents to recognize and support their emerging adult's increasing autonomy, self-sufficiency, and competence
- The ongoing significance of parents as the primary role models for their sons and daughters throughout the life span

We conclude by offering our most heartfelt wish and hope that you, the readers, will be among the very proud parents who have the enormous pleasure of watching their son or daughter graduate from college as a competent, resilient, intellectually curious, and optimistic young adult. We know that your contribution as a parent to your student's success and emotional wellness will go a long way toward making this wish a reality.

Notes

INTRODUCTION

1. American College Health Association, "College Health Assessment Spring 2008 Reference Group Data Report (Abridged)," *Journal of American College Health* 57 (2009): 485; V. Barr, R. Rando, B. Krylowicz, and D. Reetz, *The Association for University and College Counseling Center Directors Annual Survey. Reporting Period: September 1, 2009 through August 31, 2010*, Association for University and College Counseling Center Directors, http://www.aucccd.org/img/pdfs/aucccd_directors_survey_monograph_2010.pdf; R. P. Gallagher, *National Survey of Counseling Center Directors, 2009*, http://www.education.pitt.edu/survey/nsccd/archive/2009/monograph.pdf; R. W. Hingson and A. M. White, "Magnitude and Prevention of College Alcohol and Drug Misuse: US College Students Aged 18–24," in *Mental Health Care in the College Community*, ed. J. Kay and V. Schwartz (Chichester, UK: Wiley Blackwell, 2010); D. Sontag, "Who Was Responsible for Elizabeth Shin?" *New York Times*, April 28, 2002, http://www.nytimes.com/2002/04/28/magazine/28MIT.html?pagewanted=all; Virginia Tech Review Panel, *Mass Shootings at Virginia Tech: Report of the Review Panel*, August 2007.

2. American College Health Association, "College Health Assessment Spring 2008 Reference Group Data Report (Abridged)"; *mtvU AP 2009 Economy, College Stress, and Mental Health Poll*, http://www.jedfoundation.org.

3. Hingson and White, "Magnitude and Prevention of College Alcohol and Drug Misuse."

4. *mtvU AP 2010 Technology and Mental Health Poll Executive Summary*, http://www.jedfoundation.org.

5. K. Carey, "U.S. College Graduation Rate Stays Pretty Much Exactly the Same," The Quick and the Ed, December 2, 2010, http://www.quickanded.com/2010/12u-s-college-graduation-rate-stays-pretty-much-exactly-the-same.html.

6. *mtvU AP 2009 Economy, College Stress, and Mental Health Poll*.

7. *mtvU AP 2010 Technology and Mental Health Poll Executive Summary*.

1. THE ROLE OF THE PARENT IN PROMOTING EMOTIONAL WELLNESS

1. K. A. Girard, "Working with Parents and Families of Young Adults," in *Mental Health Care in the College Community*, ed. J. Kay and V. Schwartz, pp. 179-202 (Chichester, UK: Wiley-Blackwell, 2010).
2. "Colleges Try to Deal with Hovering Parents," *New York Times*, August 28, 2005, http://www.nytimes.com/aponline/national/AP-College-Helicopter-Parents.html.
3. Family Educational Rights and Privacy Act (FERPA) (20 U.S.C. § 1232g; 34 CFR Part 99), http://www2.ed.gov/policy/gen/guid/fpco/ferpa/index.html.
4. Health Insurance Portability and Accountability Act of 1996 (HIPAA), Public Law 104-191, http://www.hhs.gov/ocr/privacy/.
5. B. Kantrowitz and P. Tyre, "The Fine Art of Letting Go," *Newsweek*, May 22, 2006, 49–58; K. L. Coburn and M. L. Treeger, *Letting Go: A Parents' Guide to Understanding the College Years*, 4th ed. (New York: HarperCollins, 2003).

2. HELPING YOUR CHILD WITH COLLEGE SELECTION AND PREPARATION

1. A. W. Astin, "Involvement in Learning Revisited: Lessons We Have Learned," *Journal of College Student Development* 37 (1996): 123–33.
2. J. R. Keup and B. O. Barefoot, "Learning How to Be a Successful Student: Exploring the Impact of First-Year Seminars on Student Outcomes," *Journal of the First-Year Experience and Students in Transition* 17 (2005): 11–47; S. R. Porter and R. L. Swing, "Understanding How First–Year Seminars Affect Persistence," *Research in Higher Education* 44 (2006): 89–109.
3. *A Pocket Guide to Choosing a College* (English version), http://nsse.iub.edu/pdf/nsse_pocketguide.pdf; *Una guia de bolsillo para escoger una universidad* (Spanish version), http://nsse.iub.edu/pdf/nsse_pocketguide.pdf_spanish.pdf.
4. S. Gregory, "Time Out: Gauging the Value of a Gap Year before College," *Time*, September 21, 2010, http://www.time.com/time/magazine/article/0,9171,2015783,00.html.

3. THE TRANSITION TO COLLEGE AND HOW PARENTS CAN HELP

1. Iona College Counseling Center website transition to college, www.iona.edu/studentlife/counsel/brochures/transition.cfm.
2. J. F. Milem and J. B. Burger, "A Modified Model of College Student Persistence: Exploring the Relationships between Astin's Theory of Involvement and Tinto's Theory of Student Departure," *Journal of College Student Development* 38 (1997): 387–400.
3. E. Erikson, *Identity and the Life Cycle* (New York: Norton, 1980).
4. B. Hofer, "Pressure to Text Mom," *New York Times*, October 11, 2010, http://www.nytimes.com/roomfordebate/2010/10/11/have-college-freshmen-changed/pressure-to-text-mom.
5. C. K. Schmidt and A. C. Welsh, "College Adjustment and Subjective Well-Being When Coping with a Family Member's Illness," *Journal of Counseling & Development* 88, (2010): 397–406.
6. G. Smith et al., *Diversity Works: The Emerging Picture of How Students Benefit* (Washington, DC: Association of American Colleges and Universities, 1997).

7. I. Grieger and S. Toliver, "Multiculturalism on Predominately White Campuses: Multiple Roles and Functions for the Counselor," in *Handbook of Multicultural Counseling*, 2nd ed., ed. J. G. Ponterotto et al. (Thousand Oaks, CA: Sage, 2001).

4. TODAY'S CAMPUS ENVIRONMENT

1. American College Health Association, "College Health Assessment Spring 2008 Reference Group Data Report (Abridged)," *Journal of American College Health* 57 (2009).
2. R. Kadison and T. DiGeronimo, *College of the Overwhelmed: The Campus Mental Health Crisis and What to Do about It* (San Francisco: Jossey-Bass, 2004).
3. "NIDA Infofacts: Drug-Related Hospital Emergency Room Visits," National Institute on Drug Abuse, 2011, http://www.nida.nih.gov/infofacts/HospitalVisits.html.
4. R. Sampson, *Acquaintance Rape of College Students: Problem-Specific Guide No. 17* (Washington, DC: U.S. Department of Justice, 2002), http://www.cops.usdoj.gov/pdf/e03031472.pdf.
5. A. Abbey, "Alcohol-Related Sexual Assault: A Common Problem among College Students," 2002, http://www.collegedrinkingprevention.gov/SupportingResearch/Journal/abbey.aspx.
6. "Campus Dating Violence Fact Sheet," Dating Violence Resource Center, 2002, http://www.ncvc.org/dvrc.
7. "Love Shouldn't Hurt," Iona College, http://www.iona.edu/studentlife/counsel.
8. "Facts about Sexual Harrassment," U.S. Equal Employment Opportunity Commission, 2002, http://www.eeoc.gov/facts/fs-sex.html.
9. *Sex and Tech: Results from a Survey of Teens and Young Adults*, The National Campaign to Prevent Teen and Unplanned Pregnancy, http://www.thenationalcampaign.org/sextech/pdf/sextech_summary.pdf.
10. "Survey Suggests 'Sexting' Rampant in College," *U.S. News and World Report*, July 21, 2011, http://healthnews.usnews.com/health-news/family-health/children-health/articles/2011/07/21.
11. "Sexting: What Is It?," A Thin Line, http://www.athinline.org/facts/sexting.
12. "Sexting: What Is It?"
13. J. Cloud, "Bullied to Death?," *Time*, October 18, 2010, 59–62.
14. "Bullying and Stalking on the College Campus: Shedding Light on Complicated Issues," AllOne Health webinar, November 18, 2011, http://www.allonehealth.com/webinars/?webinar=Bullying.
15. Definitions: cyberbullying, cyberstalking, cyber harassment, invasion of privacy, from "Cyber Safety Glossary," Government of South Australia, http://www.schools.sa.gov.au/speced2/pages/cybersafety/36277/?reFlag=1.
16. E. Allan and M. Madden, "Hazing in View: College Students at Risk," Initial Finding from the National Study of Student Hazing, 2008, http://www.hazingstudy.org/publication/hazing_in_view_web.pdf.
17. Allan and Madden, "Hazing in View."
18. G. Deisinger, M. Randazzo, D. O'Neil, and J. Savage, *The Handbook for Campus Threat Assessment and Management Teams* (Boston: Applied Risk Management, 2008).

5. RECOGNIZING SIGNS OF PSYCHOLOGICAL PROBLEMS, CHEMICAL DEPENDENCY, AND ADDICTIVE BEHAVIOR

1. American College Health Association, "College Health Assessment Spring 2008 Reference Group Data Report (Abridged)," *Journal of American College Health* 57 (2009): 485; R.

Kadison and T. DiGeronimo, *College of the Overwhelmed: The Campus Mental Health Crisis and What to Do about It* (San Francisco: Jossey-Bass, 2004); T. Gabriel, "Serious Mental Health Needs Seen Growing at Colleges," *New York Times*, December 20, 2010, http://www.nytimes.com/2010/12/20/health/20campus.html.

2. American Psychiatric Association, *Diagnostic and Statistical Manual of Mental Disorders*, 4th ed. (Arlington, VA: American Psychiatric Association, 2000); "Depression," National Institute of Mental Health, http://www.nimh.nih.gov/health/topics/depression/index.shtml.

3. J. Preston and J. Johnson, *Clinical Psychopharmacology Made Ridiculously Simple*, 5th ed. (Miami, FL: MedMaster, 2007); R. Manber et al., "Faster Remission of Chronic Depression with Combined Psychotherapy and Medication Than with Each Therapy Alone," *Journal of Consulting and Clinical Psychology* 76 (2008): 459–67.

4. "Warning Signs and Risk Factors of Suicide," Yellow Ribbon Suicide Prevention Program, 2011, http://www.yellowribbon.org/WarningSigns.html.

5. A. A. D'Onofrio, *Adolescent Self-Injury: A Comprehensive Guide for Counselors and Health Care Professionals* (New York: Springer, 2007).

6. American Psychiatric Association, *Diagnostic and Statistical Manual of Mental Disorders*.

7. C. Tucker-Ladd, "Anger and Aggression," in *Psychological Self-Help*, ch. 7, 1997, http://www.psychologicalselfhelp.org/.

8. American Psychological Association, *Stress in America Report*, 2010, http://www.apa.org/news/press/release/stress/national-report.pdf.

9. American Psychiatric Association, *Diagnostic and Statistical Manual of Mental Disorders*; National Institute of Mental Health, "Anxiety Disorders," http://www.nimh.nih.gov/health/topics/anxiety-disorders/index.shtml.

10. Preston and Johnson, *Clinical Psychopharmacology Made Ridiculously Simple*.

11. American Psychiatric Association, *Diagnostic and Statistical Manual of Mental Disorders*; National Institute of Mental Health, "Schizophrenia," http://www.nimh.nih.gov/health/topics/schizophrenia/index.shtml.

12. Preston and Johnson, *Clinical Psychopharmacology Made Ridiculously Simple*.

13. National Institute of Mental Health "Bipolar Disorder," http//www.nimh.nih.gov/health/topics/bipolar-disorder/index.shtml.

14. Preston and Johnson, *Clinical Psychopharmacology Made Ridiculously Simple*.

15. National Institute of Mental Health, "Eating Disorders," http://www.nimh.nih.gov/health/publications/eating-disorders/complete-index.shtml.

16. A. Kingsbury, "Toward a Safer Campus," *U.S. News and World Report*, April 30, 2007, 48–52.

17. National Institute on Alcohol Abuse and Alcoholism, *A Call to Action: Changing the Culture of Drinking at U.S. Colleges*, 2002, http://www.collegedrinkingprevention.gov/media/TaskForceReport.pdf.

18. "DrugFacts: Drug-Related Hospital Emergency Room Visits," National Institute on Drug Abuse, http://www.drugabuse.gov/publications/drugfacts/drug-related-hospital-emergency-room-visits.

19. "FDA Calls 7 Caffeine-Alcohol Drinks Unsafe," CNN, November 17, 2010, http://www.cnn.com/2010/HEALTH/11/17/alcohol.caffeine.drinks/index.html?iref=storysearch.

20. "Prescription Drugs," Higher Education Center for Alcohol and Other Drug Abuse and Violence Prevention, http://www.highered.center.org.

21. "DrugFacts: Prescription and Over-the-Counter Medications," National Institute on Drug Abuse, http://www.drugabuse.gov/publications/drugfacts/prescription-over-counter-medications.

22. "DrugFacts: Prescription and Over-the-Counter Medications."

23. M. Trudeau, "More Students Turning Illegally to Smart Drugs," 2009, http://www.npr.org/templates/story/story.php?storyId=100254163; A. Jacobs, "The Adderall Advantage," *New York Times*, July 31, 2005, http://www.nytimes.com/2005/07/31/education/edlife/jacobs31.html; L. Carroll, "Steroids for School: College Students Get Hooked on 'Smart Drugs,'" MSNBC, May 17, 2011, http//today.msnbc.msn.com/id/43050779/ns/today-to-day_health/t/steroids-school-college-students-get-hooked-smart-drugs/#.T8t7xs1Qhbw.

24. Unless otherwise noted, information on illegal drugs is drawn from "DrugFacts," National Institute on Drug Abuse, http://www.drugabuse.gov/publications/term/160/DrugFacts.
25. M. McMillen, "Bath Salts Drug Trend: Expert Q & A," *Web*MD, June 3, 2012, http://www.webmd.com/mental-health/features/bath-salts-drug-dangers; J. Halladay, "States Race to Ban Risky 'Bath Salts' Drug," *USA Today*, February 11, 2011, http://www.usatoday.com/yourlife/health/2011-02-11-bathsalts11_ST_N.htm.
26. S. Par, "K2/Spice Fact Sheet," Community Coalitions of Virginia, 2010, http://www.ccova.org; "DEA Makes Synthetic Marijuana a Schedule 1 Drug," Addiction Inbox, March 2, 2011, http://addition-dirkh.blogspot.com/2011/03/spice-k-2-other-fake-pot-illegal-as-of.html.
27. S. Friess, "Colleges Often Turn a Blind Eye to Student Gambling Problems," *New York Times*, October 2, 2009, http://thechoice.blogs.nytimes.com/tag/gambling-addiction/.
28. "Pathological Gambling: Treatments Are Based on Those Used to Treat Addiction," *Harvard Mental Health Letter* 27 (2010): 1–3.
29. "Protecting Your Child's Mental Health: What Can Parents Do?" Jed Foundation, 2011, http://www.jedfoundation.org/parents.

6. CAMPUS SERVICES AND RESOURCES

1. For example, see the websites of Iona College, Counseling Center (http://www.iona.edu/studentlife/counsel/index.cfm) and the University of Virgina, Elson Student Health Center (http://www.virginia.edu/studenthealth/peer/info).
2. Canisius College, Office of Student Success and Retention, http://www.canisius.edu/retention/; Iona College, Office of Student Retention, http://www.iona.edu/studentlife/studentretention/.
3. Fordham University, Health Center, http://www.fordham.edu/campus_resources/student_services/student_health_servi/.
4. Gordie Center for Alcohol and Substance Education at the University of Virginia, http://www.virginia.edu/case/; Fordham University. Available at: http://www.fordham.edu/student_affairs/deans_of_students_an/student_handbooks/graduate_guide/university_offices/the_alcohol_and_othe_79392.asp.
5. Iona College, Residential Life, http://www.iona.edu/studentlife/residentiallife/.
6. University of Virginia, Accessibility Information for Students, Faculty, and Staff, http://www.virginia.edu/accessibility; Iona College, College Assistance Program, http://www.iona.edu/acedemic/support/cap/index.cfm.
7. Americans with Disabilities Act Amendments Act of 2008, U.S. Equal Employment Opportunity Commission, http://www.eeoc.gov/laws/statutes/adaaa_info.cfm.
8. Fordham University, Office of Multicultural Affairs, http://www.fordham.edu/student_affairs/mulitcultural_affair/oma_mission_30355.asp; University of Kansas, Office of Multicultural Affairs, http://www.oma.ku.edu; Columbia University, Office of Multicultural Affairs, http://www.studentaffairs.columbia.edu/multicultural.
9. Iona College, Office of Campus Ministries, http://www.iona.edu/studentlife/ministry/.
10. Fordham University, International Student Office, http://www.fordham.edu/student_affairs/student_services/special_programs/office_of_internatio/index.asp.
11. Iona College, Samuel Rudin Academic Resource Center, http://www.iona.edu/academic/support; Fordham University International Student Office.
12. Iona College, Gerri Ripp Center for Career Development, http://www.iona.edu/studentlife/career/.
13. Iona College, Office of Student Development, http://www.iona.edu/studentlife/student-development/.
14. University of Virginia, *Handbook for Parents*, http://www.virginia.edu/vpsa/parentshandbook.pdf.
15. Iona College, Office of Student Financial Services, http://www.iona.edu/admin/sfs/; University of Virginia Student Financial Services, http://www.virginia.edu/financialaid/.

16. Iona College, Office of Campus Safety and Security, http://www.iona.edu/studentlife/safety/.
17. University of Texas at Austin, Office of Ombudsperson, http://www.utexas.edu/student/ombuds/help.html; University of Chicago, Office of the Student Ombudsperson, http://ombudsperson.uchicago.edu/.

7. PROMOTING EMOTIONAL WELLNESS AND STUDENT SUCCESS

1. R. Kadison and T. DiGeronimo, *College of the Overwhelmed: The Campus Mental Health Crisis and What to Do about It* (San Francisco: Jossey-Bass, 2004).
2. Kadison and DiGeronimo, *College of the Overwhelmed*.
3. M. Davis, E. R. Eshelman, and M. McKay, *The Relaxation and Stress Reduction Workbook*, 5th ed. (Oakland, CA: New Harbinger, 2000).
4. D. Burns, *Feeling Good: The New Mood Therapy* (New York: Avon Books, 1999).
5. Burns, *Feeling Good*; D. Burns, *The Feeling Good Handbook* (New York: Plume, 1999); D. Burns, *Why Panic Attacks: The New Drug-Free Anxiety Therapy That Can Change Your Life* (New York: Broadway Books, 2006).
6. M. E. P. Seligman, *Authentic Happiness: Using the New Positive Psychology to Realize Your Potential for Lasting Fulfillment* (New York: Free Press, 2002); M. E. P. Seligman and M. Csikszentmihalyi, "Positive Psychology: An Introduction," *American Psychologist* 55 (2000): 5–14.
7. C. Wallis, "The New Science of Happiness," *Time*, January 9, 2005, http://www.time.com/time/magazine/article/0,9171,1015902,00.html.
8. "Dad's Good Parenting May Help Daughters Avoid Risky Sex," Medline Plus, June 2011, http://www.nlm.nih.gov/medlineplus/news/fullstory_113340.html.
9. The BACCHUS Network, http://bacchusnetwork.org/; Active Minds on Campus, http://www.activeminds.org/; Step Up!, http://www.stepupprogram.org/; Green Dot, http://www.livethegreendot.com/.
10. Iona College, Respect Campaign, http://www.iona.edu/studentlife/counsel/guide/respectcampaign.cfm.
11. Kadison and DiGeronimo, *College of the Overwhelmed*.
12. Kadison and DiGeronimo, *College of the Overwhelmed*.
13. M. E. Pritchard and G. S. Wilson, "Using Emotional and Social Factors to Predict Student Success," *Journal of College Student Development* 44 (2003): 18–28; L. A. Schreiner, *Linking Student Satisfaction and Retention* (Iowa City, IA: Noel-Levitz, 2009).
14. Iona College, *Success and Survival Guide*, 2011, http://www.iona.edu/studentlife/counsel/brochures/index.cfm.
15. ULifeline, http://www.iona.edu/studentlife/counsel/brochures/index.cfm; The Jed Foundation, http://www.jedfoundation.org/; The Trevor Project, http://www.thetrevorproject.org/; It Gets Better Project, http://www.itgetsbetter.org/.
16. D. Sontag, "Who Was Responsible for Elizabeth Shin?" *New York Times*, April 28, 2002, http://www.nytimes.com/2002/04/28/magazine/28MIT.html?pagewanted=all; Virginia Tech Review Panel, *Mass Shootings at Virginia Tech: Report of the Review Panel*, August 2007; S. A. Benton et al., "Changes in Counseling Client Problems across Thirteen Years," *Professional Psychology Research and Practice* 34 (2003): 68–72.

CONCLUSION

1. A. P. Carnevale, "For a Middle Class Life, College Is Crucial," *New York Times*, March 1, 2012, http://www.nytimes.com/roomfordebate/2012/03/01/should-college-be-for-everyone/for-a-middle-class-life-college-is-crucial; T. Cowen, "Graduates' Pay Is Slipping, but Still Outpaces Others," *New York Times*, March 1, 2012, http://nytimes.com/roomfordebate/2012/03/01/should-college-be-for-everyone/college-pay-is-slipping-but-still-outpaces-others.

Index

Abilify, 87
abusive relationships, 2, 16
academic advisors, 130
academic challenges, 39–42; assisting with, 40–42
academic dishonesty, 41
academic reputation, 20
academic resources, 24, 40; office of, 130
academic support services, 114; office of disabilities/learning needs, 114
advisors, academic, 48
aggression, 83–84
alcohol abuse, 92–93, 93; impact of, 93, 94; assistance with, 94–95; caffeinated alcohol beverage, 95
alcohol and other drugs, 60, 91–102
alcohol and other drug (AOD) services, 102, 110; office of, 131
American Psychological Association (APA), 46
Americans with Disabilities Act Amendments Act (ADAAA), 26, 112
anger, 83–84; management of, 84; signs of, 84
anti-anxiety medications, 86
anti-depression medications, 79; Celexa, 79; Effexor, 79; Lexapro, 79; Prozac, 79; Zoloft, 79
anti-psychotic medications, 87; Abilify, 87; Haldol, 87; Risperdal, 87; Seroquel, 87; Zyprexa, 87

anxiety, 2, 6, 34, 51, 86; assistance with, 86; types of, 86
attention deficit disorder, 2, 96
autonomy, 9, 11, 12

balance, 129
bias incidents, 74
bi-cultural stress, 45
binge-drinking, 2, 60
bipolar disorder, 88; symptoms of, 88; treatment of, 88
bullying, 2, 6, 16, 71
Burns, David, M.D., 123
Bystander Intervention Training, 72, 127

campus culture, 24–25, 54
campus environment, 53, 57–76, 132
campus housing, 25
campus ministries, 113
Campus Prevention Elimination Act, 61
campus safety and security, 116–117
campus size, 22–23
campus visit, 17, 28–30; questions to ask, 29–30
career decisions, 47–49; assisting with, 48–49; choosing a major, 47–48, 54
career development services, 48, 115
Celexa, 79
chemical dependency, 6, 16, 51, 91–102; assisting with, 101–102; signs of, 100–101, 103–104

Cleary Act, 75, 117
co-curricular activities, 26–27, 49
Cognitive Behavioral Therapy (CBT), 123
College Board, 19
college counselors, 4
College Parents of America, 19
college professionals, 53; administrators, 4, 25; faculty, 4, 23, 25, 48, 52
college selection, 3, 5, 17–35; getting started, 18–19; factors to consider, 20–28
communication, 119–121; parents/student, 119–121; cultural differences, 121; tips for, 121
confidentiality, 10, 13–14
coping skills, 122–123
counseling center, 44, 47, 52, 66, 78, 79, 105–108, 125; benefits of, 107–108, 131
Counseling and Psychological Services (CAPS), 105–106, 131; assisting with referral, 107–108; confidentiality, 106
cultural challenges, 52–53; assisting with, 53
cultural differences, 12, 45, 47
culture, definition of, 52
curriculum, 23–24
cyber-bullying, 2, 6, 71–72; assistance with, 72–73
cyberspace, 69–71

date rape, 60–65; assisting with, 62–63
date rape drugs, 63–65; assisting with, 64–65
Depakote, 88
depression, 2, 6, 34, 51, 58–59, 78–79; causes of, 78; symptoms of, 79; treatment for, 79
developmental concerns, 3, 5; identity development, 44–47
disabilities/learning needs, office of, 111–112; American With Disabilities-Amended Act, 112
diversity, 24–25, 51, 52–53; multicultural office, 112–113; international students, 114
divorce, 51

eating disorders, 2, 6, 34, 88–90; symptoms of, 88; causes of, 90; impact of media on, 88; parental role in, 89, 90; types of, anorexia nervosa, 89; bulimia, 89; binge eating, 89
Effexor, 79
emergency notification system, 117
emerging adult, 44, 46, 47, 50, 119
employment, on campus, 49
engagement, 21, 27, 39, 115
Erikson, Erik, 45
exhaustion, 2, 129
expectations, of college students, 12–13

family, problems, 51–52; assisting with, 50; divorce, 51; illness, 51
FERPA (Family Educational Rights and Privacy Act), 13, 14, 116
finances, 2, 21–22; challenges of, 40, 41, 51, 54
first generation, college student, 45
first-year experience, 27–28, 38, 39
first year, importance of, 37–39, 130

gambling, addiction to, 102–103
gaming, compulsive, 102–103
gap year, 32
generalized anxiety disorder, 86
graduation rates, 2, 20, 37
grief, 82–83

Haldol, 87
happiness, cultivating, 125–126
harassment, peers, 2, 16
hazing, 73
health services, 109
helicopter parent, 11
high school professionals, counselors, 4, 16, 17, 19, 33–34, 35; teachers, 4, 16, 17, 19, 35
HIPAA (Health Insurance Portability and Accountability Act), 13
homesickness, 42, 54

identify development, 44–47; assisting with, 46–47; identity crisis, 45
illegal drugs, 97–100; cocaine, 97; ecstasy, 97; heroine, 98; PCP, 99; marijuana, 97; steroids, 99; bath salts, 100; spice/

K2, 100; psilocybin mushroom, 98; LSD, 99; methamphetamine, 98
ItGetsBetter.org, 131
in loco parentis, 58
international students office, 114
internship, 48, 49

Jed Foundation, 131

learning needs, 111
leave of absence, 55
Lexapro, 79
lifestyle choices encouraging healthy choices, 128–129; exercise, 128; healthy weight and eating habits, 128; stress reduction, 128
Lithium, 88
living arrangements, 49–50; assisting with, 50; at home, 50; on campus, 49, 50, 58
location, of campus, 22
loneliness, 42

majors, 130
mental health, crisis, 2, 58–59
mentor, 53
millennial generation, 10
mood stabilizers, 88; Depakote,5.130; Lithium, 88
multicultural affairs, office of, 112–113

National College Health Association, 58

Obsessive Compulsive Disorder (OCD), 86
Ombudsperson, office of, 117–118
orientation, 38, 118
outreach services, 131
overview, of chapters, 5–7

panic disorder, 86
parents, as sources of help, 3, 5, 7, 9–11; expectations,3.58; letting go, 14–13; parent/child relationship, 15; resources for, 17, 19, 20, 21
parents handbook, 115
peer educators, 110, 127
persistence, 3, 37
PFLAG (Parents, Families and Friends of Lesbians and Gays), 46

phobias, 86
post traumatic stress disorder (PTSD), 86
positive psychology, 125–126
prescription drugs, abuse of, 2, 6, 95–96; assisting with, 85; opiode/pain killers, 95; stimulants, 96; depressant, central nervous system (CNS), 96
prescription medication, compliance with, 129
privacy, 10, 13–14; in cyberspace, 71
protective factors, 3
Prozac, 79
psychological problems, 2, 6, 16, 18, 22, 33, 41; pre-existing, 33–34, 54, 59; continuity of services, 33, 59
psychiatric/psychological referrals, availability of, 33–34
psychosis and schizophrenia, 87; with bi-polar disorder, 79

readiness, for college, 17, 30–33
relationships, abusive, 65; assisting with, 66; healthy, signs of, 65–66; unhealthy, signs of, 66, 129
resident assistant (RA), 43, 58, 111
residential life, office of, 111
retention, 20, 37; office of, 108–109
Risperdal, 87
roommate conflicts, 68–69; assisting with, 69

safe sex, 128–129
safety, assisting with, 75–76
schizophrenia, 87; signs of, 87; treatment of, 87
seasonal affective disorder (SAD), 22
self-defeating thoughts, 123–124
self-esteem, 126; building, 126–127
self-injury, 2, 13, 80–81
self-respect, 126; building, 126–127
Seligman, Martin, 125
separation anxiety, 42–44; assisting with, 43–44
Seroquel, 87
sexting, 69–70
sexual assault, 60–65
sexual harassment, 67–68; assisting with, 67–68; ombudsperson, 68

sexual orientation, 45; It Gets Better, 131; The Trevor Project, 131
signature strengths, 125
sleep, 129
special needs, 25–26, 53; learning disabilities, 41; services for, 111–112
spirituality, 25, 127; campus ministries, 113
stress, 2, 51, 84–85, 85; causes of, 84–85
student affairs, office of, 115
student handbook, 115
student financial services, 116
student retention, office of, 108–109, 131
student services, 6, 26, 27, 41, 118; types of, 118; learning about, 118, 132; advocating for, 132
students of concern committee, 74, 90
success, promotion of, 6, 37, 39; factors of, 130–132
suicide, thoughts of, 2, 59, 80; warning signs, 80
supervision, 2, 58

terrorism, 2, 82, 117

The Trevor Project, 131
thought disorders, 2
threat assessment teams, 74, 90
transfer, to another college, 5, 16, 17–35, 55
transgender, 45, 46
transition, to college, 3, 5, 34; assisting with, 54–55; struggles with, 37–55
trauma, 82–83; assisting with, 82–83; reaction to, 82
troubled students, 90–91; signs of, 91; treatment of, 91

Ulifeline (Jed Foundation), 131
unhealthy choices, 1
U.S. News & World Report, 17, 20

violence, 2, 6, 74–76; assisting with,4.167-4.171
volunteering, 113, 127

Zoloft, 79
Zyprexa, 87

About the Authors

Diana Trevouledes, PhD, is a New York State–licensed clinical psychologist and social worker. She is currently a faculty member in the departments of psychology and public health at St. Louis University, Madrid Campus, Spain. Prior to her position at St. Louis University, Dr. Trevouledes was program director for the masters of science in mental health counseling at Mercy College, New York, and coordinator of counseling and psychological services at Fordham University, Marymount Campus, New York. She attended Adelphi University (PhD, clinical psychology) and New York University (MSW, clinical social work). Dr. Trevouledes has held faculty positions at Fordham University, Mercy College, and the City University of New York, teaching psychology and mental health counseling at the doctoral, masters, and undergraduate levels. She has over twenty years of clinical experience that encompasses a variety of mental health settings including inpatient, outpatient, partial hospital, psychiatric emergency room, university counseling centers, and private practice.

Ingrid Grieger, EdD, has been director of the counseling center at Iona College in New Rochelle, New York, since 1989 and has served as a founding member and chair of the Student Development Diversity Committee. She is also an adjunct associate professor in the Department of Psychology at Iona College and an adjunct professor in the Graduate School of Education at Fordham University. Dr. Grieger received her doctorate in counseling from the University of Virginia. Since that time she has worked in a number of college and university counseling centers, including the University of Virginia and Bowling Green State University, in community mental health clinics, and in private clinical practice. She has been a frequent presenter at professional conferences and has published extensively in the areas of women's issues in psychotherapy, multicultural concerns, organizational development, and innovative programming and systemic interventions in student affairs. For twenty years, Dr. Grieger has made presentations to the parents of first-year students regarding the challenges and joys of making the successful transition from high school to college.

www.ingramcontent.com/pod-product-compliance
Lightning Source LLC
Chambersburg PA
CBHW020741230426
43665CB00009B/519